GUIDE FOR THE

MODERN
BEAR

A FIELD STUDY of BEARS in the WILD

By Travis Smith and Chris Bale

Photography by Leland Gebhardt

Illustration by Jason Hill

Paul
Wolfy
Woofs

XO
Chris

To Paul!
Thanks for the
FAB Photos!
Big Bear Hugs!
Travis Smith

For Marilyn "Mike" Keller

Thank you for always believing in "TNT"
and helping to make Modern Bear a reality.

Copyright © 2014
Chris Bale and Travis Smith, Modern Bear Media
www.facebook.com/modernbear
www.modernbear.net

ISBN: 978-0-9851871-7-0

Printed in the USA

Contents

Foreward

By Bill Sanderson

What is a bear? I wish I could count how many times I have been asked that question. Once, during a birthday party with ten bear friends at a suburban restaurant, a straight woman approached our table and asked, "What group are you?" The general public sees a group of men with beards and is curious why they are hanging out together. My partner Andy and I get routinely questioned: "Are you brothers?" People see we have a connection between us. We have been domestic partners for twenty years but the "gay" idea never enters their mind. The matching beards seem to throw them for a curve!

My definition of a bear: A gay man who is comfortable in his own body type whether he has a 30 inch waist from twenty hours at the gym, or a 48 inch waist from twenty hours of couch potato curls. He is accepting of others and not judgmental of his brother bears. Beard and body hair are a plus but not always required.

I liked bears long before the term "Bear" was coined. When I first discovered ABBA's *Arrival* album it was Benny Andersson's bearded face that drew me to the cover. I knew he was my type even in my teen years. If you are still challenged visualizing what a bear is, think of the character Al from the TV show *Home Improvement*. The Al character had the classic bear look.

The bear community has been a large part of my life. I have many bear friends. There are bear bars, bear authors, bear music groups, bear contests, bear dances, bear travel groups, and many bear websites.

Back in 1991, I won "Mr. Bear New England". Winning that title inspired me to create the NEB (New England Bears) club, where we met monthly at The Ramrod in Boston. Before there was Facebook or Twitter, MySpace or blogs, I started a website called BigMuscleBears.com. The idea was that if you were big or muscular or a bear, you were welcome to join, and bear admirers were welcome too.

The bear community is as diverse as any other sub culture or group. It is constantly changing and forming new groups. I have even seen a few women that call themselves bears!

Recently, Modern Bear has caught everyone's attention for its appealing postmodern view of the world using a bear focused lens.

Guide for the Modern Bear gleefully leads us through this world, taking us inside the lives and homes of the characters that inhabit it. The *Guide* playfully answers the question of 'what is a modern bear?' expanding definitions with humor, colorful photos, and inside information on where to eat, live, and play. I look forward to taking this handy *Guide* to P-Town during Bear Week. How cool will it be to spot one of the critters while lounging at the beach and be able to look up his likes and interests? It will certainly be a conversation starter!

Bill Sanderson
Owner & Creator of BigMuscleBears.com
Former Mr. Bear New England

"Be nice - it is the Bear thing to do!"

How I Stopped Worrying and Embraced My Inner Bear

I was a Bear and didn't know it. I had no idea the Bear community existed until the late '90s when I "stumbled" across a most intriguing website, BigMuscleBears.com. Then and there, I realized that I belonged to this very special group of men who were furry, sexy and confidently Gay. By golly, I was a Bear! WOOF.

I was stocky (ok, chubby) and rather hirsute, things i had always been embarrassed about as a young, gay man in the '80s. I vividly remember my years of Dexatrim dieting and body shaving, desperately trying to fit the mold of the GQ models who were considered to be the personification of the Gay ideal. Pretending I was a Twink was exhausting and I eventually let nature take its furry, beefy course.

By the '90s, my once-full head of hair was noticeably thinning, so I did what I considered to be the most practical thing and shaved it all off. Major problem—with a hairless dome and a cheeky, baby face, I looked like an oversized infant. To compensate, I grew a mustache and goatee.

What I didn't know at the time was that I was inadvertently creating for myself a classic Bear look, a look that would prove to be quite popular. Who knew? I still had no idea that furry, plus-sized men were considered sex symbols within this undiscovered world. And that's when I had my momentous encounter with BigMuscleBears.com.

Queue the Angelic Choir.

Once I discovered the Bear community, I learned there was more to being a Bear than just having a certain look; there is an entire lifestyle of Bearness. There are Bear bars, Bear discos, Bear Runs, Bear websites, Bear cruises, clothing lines, toys, magazines, a lexicon and language, and so much more. I learned that the Bear community was wonderfully inclusive and welcoming, and I finally felt like I fit in. I wasn't judged because the label on my 501s said 38x30 and not the other way around. My midriff would never sport a six-pack; it featured a Bear belly, plumped by six-packs! And that was OK. I made friends. I fell in love. Life was good.

This gradual self-awakening lead to the most significant lesson of all—Bear is a state of mind.

In our *Guide for the Modern Bear*, we explore the beauty and diversity of the Modern Bear Family. Think of it as your field guide to the characters and their habitats; how they live, how they work, and the many ways they play. We focus on fourteen "animals" of the Modern Bear world so that you may gain better insight into these magnificent creatures and the environs they call home.

Now put on your favorite flannel, grab yourself a beer (or milkshake), and get ready to experience your inner Bear! All together now, "GRRRRRR."

Big Bear Hugs,

Travis Smith
Modern Bear

I Was a Teenage Wolf

As a youngster, I was inexplicably drawn to the film *An American Werewolf in London*. Later, in high school, I saw *Teen Wolf* an embarrassing number times. I swear I tingle at the sight of a full moon and have always imagined my hands getting hairy and turning into paws just like Michael J. Fox's. I joined Team Jacob by the middle of the first *Twilight* movie (a guilty pleasure if only for the hot wolves at odds with the sparkly vampires—Gay metaphor anyone?). Fantasies or not, these experiences guided my evolution from a fledgling Pup into a confident Design Wolf. As a grown man, the Wolf moniker and the Bear "type" fit me perfectly.

I first became aware of the Bear community when I joined BigMuscleBears.com and created my first-ever online profile in 2002. I didn't really identify as a "big muscle bear," but I wanted to fish in the pond of men I was attracted to. Fortunately, the Bear community sports a pretty inclusive attitude, much more accepting than the gay world I knew working in the West Hollywood area of Los Angeles, where Calvin Klein model types were the ideal and the norm. But I wasn't just a Bear appreciator—I was welcomed as an integral part of the fun and furry world of Bears, Otters, and Wolves.

For *Guide for the Modern Bear* I had hoped to find great historical references to the Bear community—I am that guy who fanatically researches everything. But historical sources were scarce, so instead, I collected anecdotes from Bears and guys and gals "adjacent" to the bear community. One recurring theme struck me as particularly interesting and important—whether or not you find Bears attractive, it is up to YOU to decide if you are a member of the Bear world. So what exactly makes a Bear? Good question!

There is a physical distinction between a man who is overweight or husky, and a burly, muscular man with some kind of fur. The first is a Chub and the second is a Bear. No matter your category, a warm, friendly attitude—more than physical traits - gets you into the club, though muscles and pelts are wildly appreciated. In the Bear world, ALL are welcome.

With our first issue of *Guide for the Modern Bear*, we celebrate a sampling of the characters found in the big, furry world of Bears. So grab your guidebook, get bear watching, and have fun exploring the spectacular variety of critters who have decided they are part of the Bear community.

You may decide you belong in our furry family! Here's hoping you do!

Enjoy!

Chris Bale
Design Wolf

MODERN BEAR

Ursus gayomous, considered the classic of the Modern Bear family, is found in both woodland and city environs throughout the Bear world.

Modern Bear tends to gravitate to densely populated areas where he can feast and frolic with the other Bears. He has created a perfect environment in the SoMa neighborhood of San Francisco in an overpriced, industrial loft, meticulously decorated with Mid Century Modern furnishings and kitschy Folk Art.

Modern Bear is known for his keen eye, collecting vintage objects and proudly displaying them in his Bear Lair. One of his favorite pastimes is bidding on vintage finds online while munching on BBQ potato chips. He has been known to hunt for hours using his favorite search words, "'50s and '60s Mid Century Modern," losing all track of time until a text or two summons him out of his cave for some fun with the other SoMa critters.

Our Modern Bear works in IT at a tech start-up, outwardly displaying both his geek and blue collar traits and behaviors. He is often seen wearing dark Levis, quirky t-shirts and flannels, black Chucks (very slimming), and prescription Ray Ban glasses. His modes of urban travel include BART, Muni and a hybrid commuter/mountain bike. With his trusty wheels, he can climb hills in the city and on the trails, keeping his meaty calves in shape for Daddy Bears to snack on.

Modern Bear's grazing habits frequently include a Super Bacon Burger and Garlic Fries at Super Duper Burger and the decadent Cowboy Roll at Barracuda Sushi. He ritually attends Friday Happy Hour at Midnight Sun and finds relaxation in long-neck Bud Lights at popular Bear watering holes like Lone Star and Truck. In these "dens" away from home, he mingles with other Bears and gossips about A-list Bear couples or the juicy "film star" who does his laundry at Brainwash. In this big, little city, everybear knows everybear.

Modern Bear's recreational activities revolve around tanning his naked hide at Baker Beach, socializing at Bears in the Park gatherings in Mission-Dolores Park, working off those potato chips at the SoMa Gold's Gym, and meeting his buds for MovieBears screenings. He often uses his city car share to visit a Bear buddy's fabulously preserved Eichler home in San Mateo. Modern Bear is saving to buy his own Eichler, a design-addict's dream setting for obsessive, mid-century decorating—and it's 20 miles closer to his dream job at Apple!

It is no secret that Modern Bear loves to forage. Whether it is vintage modern furniture at Past Perfect in the Marina or bottle cap collectibles at the Alemany Flea Market, he is always on the hunt for the ultimate score. His clothing store of choice is Unionmade where he finds the perfect pair of jeans that look like they were worn by an old prospector, yet accentuate Modern Bear's burly ass.

Coffee fuels this bear and his adventures so he regularly treks to "Bearbucks" on 18th Street in the Castro, or Piccino in the Dogpatch when he's craving a "single origin" cup of locally roasted Sightglass joe.

For his local getaway pleasures, Modern Bear trots to nearby Guerneville for Lazy Bear Weekend on the Russian River, and to Sonoma for wine tastings and scenic bike rides. Every summer, Modern Bear makes a July migration to Provincetown, MA for fun and adventure at Bear Week. He also frequents Palm Springs, CA and is spotted annually, palling around with Tiki Bear, at the ultimate MB experience, Modernism Week.

Modern Bear's mating pattern can be categorized as serial monogamy; he's searching for the ultimate Husbear. His vision of a perfect wedding day features MB and his man exchanging vows in matching his & his Tom Ford tuxedos, their guests dressed in black against white, linen-covered tables with lush, red centerpieces, all outdoors on a beautiful vineyard in Napa Valley.

Are you his potential cake-topper?

> I'm really a princess trapped in the body of a truck driver.

1. Overpriced t-shirt from Provincetown Bear Week
2. Vintage Apple iPad®
3. "Bearbucks" iced venti Caramel Macchiato; skinny, no whip
4. Ray Ban® eyewear
5. Brown Sugar Cinnamon Pop-Tarts®
6. Barbecue flavored Pringles®

7. '70s Harvest gold Funnel fireplace from Past Perfect
8. Hand-crafted log chair found at an estate sale
9. "Bear in Underwear" plush toy
10. '60s Metal wall sculpture won on eBay®
11. Big Bear Campground pillow from Target®

Cycling in the Presidio, Modern Bear takes advantage of a sunny day to burn off some tater tots.

Food & Drink

Turkey Sloppy Joe sandwich (Mom's recipe)

Tater Tots with Bob's Big Boy® Thousand Island dressing

Stewart's® Root Beer float with vanilla ice cream

Vintage tablecloth from MB's collection

LIKES: Updated comfort food!
DISLIKES: Vertical food

SAN FRANCISCO

BARS

1) Lone Star: 1354 Harrison St • (415) 863-9999 • lonestarsf.com
2) Midnight Sun: 4067 18th St • (415) 861-4186 • midnightsunsf.com
3) Truck: 1900 Folsom St • (415) 252-0306 • trucksf.com

FOOD

4) Bar Agricole: 355 11th St • (415) 355-9400 • baragricole.com
5) Barracuda Sushi: 2251 Market St • (415) 558-8567 • barracudasushi.com
6) Frances: 3870 17th St • (414) 621-3870 • frances-sf.com
7) House of Prime Rib: 1906 Van Ness Ave • (415) 885-4605 • houseofprimerib.net
8) Super Duper Burger: 2304 Market St • (415) 558-8123 • superdupersf.com

COFFEE

9) Piccino: 1001 Minnesota St • (415) 824-4224 • piccinocafe.com
10) Starbucks Castro: "Bearbucks" • 4094 18th St • (415) 626-6263 • starbucks.com

FURNITURE

11) Another Time: 1710 Market St • (415) 553-8900 • anothertimesf.com
12) Kenneth Wingard: 2319 Market St • (415) 431-6900 • kennethwingard.com
13) Modern Artifacts: 1639 Market St • (415) 400-5111 • modernartifacts.net
14) Past Perfect: 2224 Union St • (415) 929-7651 • pastperfectsf.com

SHOPPING

15) Alemany Flea Market: 100 Alemany Blvd • (415) 647-2043
16) JCPenney: 63 Serramonte Center, Daly City • (650) 731-3401 • jcpenney.com
17) Unionmade: 493 Sanchez St • (415) 861-3373 • unionmadegoods.com
18) Sonoma Nesting Co: 16151 Main St. Guerneville • (707) 869-3434 • sonomanesting.com

POINTS OF INTEREST

19) Golds Gym SOMA: 1001 Brannan St • (415) 552-4653
    goldsgym.com/sanfranciscosomaca
20) Mission-Dolores Park: 18th St to 20th St between Church and Dolores
    sfrecpark.org/missiondolorespark.aspx
21) Apple World Headquarters: 1-6 Infinite Loop, Cupertino • (408) 974-5050 • apple.com
22) Bardessono Hotel & Spa: 6526 Yount St, Yountville • (707) 204-6000 • bardessono.com
23) Guerneville: Home of Lazy Bear Weekend
24) Napa: Gorgeous wine country 50 miles NE of San Francisco • outinthevineyard.com
25) The Highlands: Largest contiguous Eichler development
    Hwy I-280 & Bunker Hill Dr, San Mateo

CLUB CUB

We find this ambitious young bear roaming the wilds of our nation's capital while working his way up the political ladder. A fledgling member of the Modern Bear world, he is a Congressional aide by day and a fun-loving circuit boy by night; or as his pals fondly call him, Club Cub.

Don't let this Cub's adorable looks fool you; his intelligence and political savvy have propelled him through the ranks on "The Hill" with lightning speed. His passion for politics started as a wee cub, running in DC's annual Halloween High Heel Drag Race as First Lady Hillary Clinton. Even at the tender age of 16, this Cub displayed confidence in himself, his progressive leanings, and his flair with a blonde wig!

A product of East Coast prep schools, this unexpected prospect for Cub-dom embraces DC's Bear culture with untamed gusto. Club Cub consciously eschews the straight Capitol Hill scene, choosing to create his personal habitat in the edgier, gayer Logan Circle neighborhood. It is here that he burrows into his frat-boy-gone-estate-sale Federalist row house.

His domestic style is a hodgepodge of rustic and vintage furniture found at Millennium and Good Wood, or "Got Wood" as he calls it, both in the U Street Corridor. Cub is the first to admit he's missing the "Gay Design Gene." He's more interested in the latest bill on the floor than the latest interior fashion trend.

To blow off steam after a hectic week in the Capital, Club Cub starts his weekend with DC Bear Crue's Happy Hour at Town. On special weekends he can be observed dancing shirtless at Blow Off, a celebrity DJ'd Bear party that pops up in cities nationwide but originated at the 9:30 Club. Sometimes, he cuts to the chase and makes a beeline for Green Lantern for some serious male hunting.

Clubbing is not the only behavior of this energetic young Bear. He often grabs an especially artistic latte at Big Bear Café to start a day of high activity, like foraging for fresh produce at the Dupont Circle Farmers' Market, admiring the latest exhibit at the National Gallery of Art, or gathering with his playmates for Movie Bears on Wednesday nights.

Our multi-faceted Club Cub is a jock too. When in outdoor mode, he is keen on canoeing the Potomac River, hiking at Great Falls or running through long, winding, and forested Rock Creek Park—a good excuse to cruise other joggers. When Cub seeks wilder thrills, he and his buds trek to King's Dominion and ride the Anaconda and the Dominator—they're roller coasters, silly! Cub's secret love is the Grizzly, an exhilarating vintage roller coaster on a wooden track through the dense Virginia forest.

A young Cub needs to eat and this critter has a bodacious appetite! A few of his favorite grazing spots include the hip American Ice Company for a Turkey or Brisket sandwich, BBQ Bus food truck for Hawaiian Pulled Pork sandwiches, and for late night grubbing, Ben's Chili Bowl for a Half-Smoke, all the way with Chili Cheese Fries. He frequents DC's own Five Guys near The Capitol when a cheeseburger and a shake are the ultimate hunger-busters during a Filibuster.

Club Cub and his beach-loving Bear buddies make pleasure trips to üBear friendly Rehoboth Beach, DE. Cub and his progressive pals forgive their Log Cabin Republican friend for his political leanings because he has a stellar, mid-century, beachfront house at Poodle Beach. Bipartisanship rules in the epicenter of Gay Rehoboth as they relax, party and dish about DC's un-Bearlievable "behind the scenes" social scene.

Cub is currently single, but perpetually on high alert for a sexy Daddy Bear with the following traits: furry, good kisser, liberal, and possessing a manly fearlessness around the barbecue. Woof!

Are you ready to fire up this Cub's grill?

How is your political pillow talk?

1. Fossil Watch
2. SKECHERS® athletic shoes
3. Wii® console for playing LEGO Star Wars®
4. Tanqueray® Gin (from the freezer) and tonic
5. *Dress Your Family in Corduroy and Denim* by David Sedaris
6. *Washington Post*, Sunday edition
7. Five Guys® burger and fries

8. Blowoff poster (Cub's favorite Bear party)
9. Grizzly Bear concert poster from the 9:30 club
10. Antique globe found at Georgetown Flea Market
11. Rustic, reclaimed-wood, coffee table from Good Wood
12. Vintage weather vane and stool from Cady's Alley shops
13) American flag (inherited from Gramps!)

Power-paddling the Potomac, Club Cub pays respect to the only Republican he loves, Abe Lincoln.

Food & Drink

Five Guys® Little Cheeseburger with Fries Five Guys Style

Fanta® orange soda

Little Debbie® Star Crunch® cookies

American flag paper plate from Mom

LIKES: Take out
DISLIKES: Extra cardio at the gym

WASHINGTON D.C.

BARS

1) 9:30 Club: 815 V St NW • (202) 265-0930 • 930.com
2) The Green Lantern: 1335 Green Ct NW • (202) 347-4533 • greenlanterndc.com
3) Town Danceboutique: 2009 8th Street NE • (202) 234-8696 • towndc.com

FOOD

4) American Ice Co: 917 V St NW • (202) 758-3562 • amicodc.com
5) Ben's Chili Bowl: 1213 U St NW • (202) 667-0909 • benschilibowl.com
6) Five Guys: 1645 Connecticut Ave NW • (202) 328-3483 • fiveguys.com
7) Georgetown Cupcake: 3301M St NW • (202) 333-8448 • georgetowncupcake.com
8) Taylor Gourmet: 1910 14th St NW • (202) 588-7117 • taylorgourmet.com
9) BBQ Bus: A roaming restaurant. Great BBQ and Comfort classics • bbqbusdc.com
   (not on map)

COFFEE

10) Big Bear Cafe: 1700 1st St NW • bigbearcafe-dc.com
11) Peregrine Espresso: 660 Pennsylvania Ave SE • (202) 629-4381• peregrineespresso.com

FURNITURE

12) Archer: 1027 33rd St NW • (202) 640-2823 • archermodern.com
13) Cady's Alley: Georgetown Design District • 3314 M Street NW • cadysalley.com
14) Good Wood: 1428 U St NW • (202) 986-3640 • goodwooddc.com
15) Millennium: 1528 U Street NW • (202) 483-1218 • millenniumdecorativearts.com
16) Modern Mobler: 7313 Georgia Avenue NW • (571) 594-2201 • modernmobler.com

SHOPPING

17) Home Rule: 1807 14th St NW • (202) 797-5544 • homerule.com
18) Junction: 1510 U St NW #B • (202) 483-0261 • junctionwdc.com
19) Kramerbooks: 1517 Connecticut Ave NW • (202) 387-1400 • kramerbooks.com

POINTS OF INTEREST

20) Barracks Row: Alternative area within the Capitol Hill neighborhood. Gay-friendly shops, restaurants, and bars • 8th St SE between E St SE and I (Eye) St SE
21) DuPont Circle FRESHFARM Market: Sundays, 20th St NW between Massachusetts Ave and Connecticut Ave • freshfarmmarket.org
22) Hollin Hills: 1940s-'50s Modern housing development designed by architect Charles Goodman • Alexadria, VA • hollinhills.net
23) Rehoboth Beach DE: The Mid-Atlantic's Key West. Over 200 LGBT-owned businesses in a small, summer resort town • Costal Hwy 1 and Rehoboth Ave
24) Rock Creek Park: One of America's first federal parks, 2000 acres of forest, creeks, and trails in the heart of DC • nps.gov/rocr

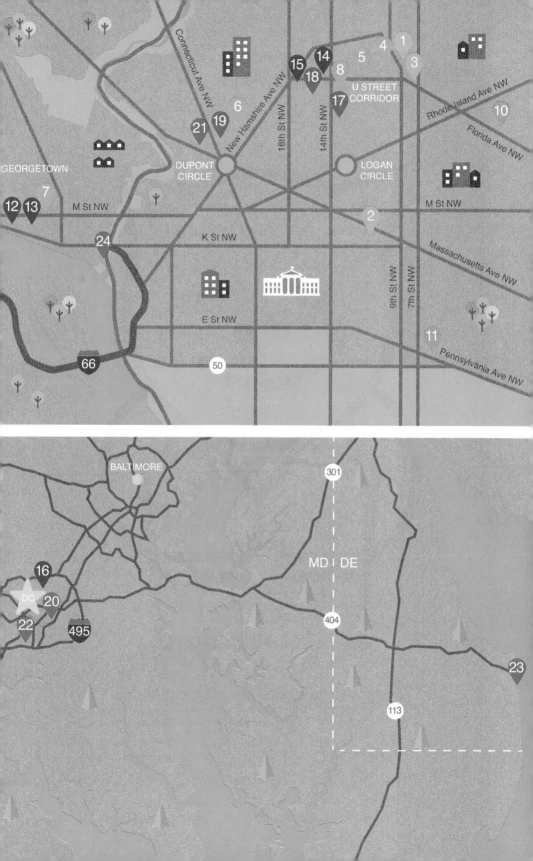

Design Wolf

With his silvery-gray beard and pelt, the striking and stoic Wolf is known as a great protector of his Bear pack, and in kind, they welcome him with open paws.

Upon hearing rumors of a rare breed of *Canis lupus*, known amongst the Bear family as Design Wolf, we searched far and wide before discovering this elusive creature in the wilderness of Manhattan Island.

Our Wolf makes his living and reputation as a successful and much-sought-after interior designer in New York City. What separates Design Wolf from others of his species is his cunning ability to hunt down the most fabulous antiques and Jonathan Adler pottery while exhibiting his impeccable fashion sense. To behold this incredible beast in full command of his environment is a true Bear delight. Watch Design Wolf prowl a Long Island City thrift store eyeing his unwitting prey, the prized Chippendale dresser, and in one stealth move—pounce—Sold!

Design Wolf frequently teams up with his best friend and protégé, Goldy Lox, to go hunting and gathering. Goldy adores helping him find clothes that accentuate his athletic form and display his silver-gray chest hair. She has been inspired by her Wolf to design custom shirts that lead viewers' eyes to his sexy tufts, and their imaginations to what mysteries lie beyond.

Unlike some of his Bear buddies, Design Wolf is especially fastidious about his appearance. Gym workouts and back-hair laser rituals guarantee prime definition of his lats and traps. To keep his svelte and muscular form, and keep pace with the water-loving Bears, Design Wolf likes to swim with Team New York Aquatics. He also has a travel membership at the David Barton gym so he can keep his pecs pumped in South Beach when he visits Goldy in her natural habitat. DW appreciates the admiring glances and cruising gestures from other animals during his summer excursions to Fire Island.

Wolves prefer to travel in packs, and Design

Wolf has many friends around the country who join him for adventurous outings. He can be found shopping in Miami with Goldy Lox, trekking the urban environs of Seattle with Panda Bear, and glamping with Modern Bear for their design rendezvous in Palm Springs. He always packs a signature vintage thermos of cool cocktails for celebratory toasts after a successful day of hunting and foraging.

For Design Wolf, it's all about the thrill of the chase. Where will he spot the most fabulous treasures for his next project? You may find him at The End of History scoping out their latest trove of Mid-Century glass decanters or at Klein Reid Studio admiring their latest ceramics collection. But our cunning Wolf keeps many of his favorite hunting grounds to himself.

At night, he retreats to his "reasonably-priced" loft in DUMBO where he surrounds himself with an eclectic collection of Bertoia furniture, fascinating found objects and ephemera, and his perfectly curated designer wardrobe.

When the moon is full, Design Wolf likes to splurge and treat himself to a Shroom Burger and a Caramel Shake at Shake Shack in Madison Square Park. He has also been spotted with his Wolf pack at Elmo in Chelsea, indulging in the Macaroni & Cheese while luxuriating in the swanky, 1960s Miami décor.

Wolves are creatures of habit and this Wolf's Sunday ritual begins with a brunch of Fried Eggs over Turkey Hash at Westville in the East Village, followed by polo shirt shopping at Ted Baker in the Meat Packing District.

When Design Wolf is feeling frisky and craving the company of a big, burly Bear, he journeys to the Bear Nights at Ty's and Rockbar in the heart of the Village. He also takes great pleasure in his visits to The Eagle rooftop where he gathers with his furry friends and soaks up the beauty of Manhattan's skylines and man-lines.

Are you daring enough to join this Wolf's pack?

Chelsea boys bore me. I'm much more interested in the stocky, dock worker type.

1. Samsung® smartphone (still misses his old Palm® Treo)
2. Collection of Jonathan Adler® vases
3. Vintage thermos collection from Chelsea Flea Market
4. Iced Mr. Brown® Blue Mountain canned coffee
5. '60s Enameled gas station number
6. James Perse® cotton sweater
7. WeSC® denim, dark blue wash
8. Modern Amusement® by Sperry® slip-on tennies
9. Eero Saarinen® Executive Armchair
10. Trader Vic's® Macadamia Nut Liqueur
11. Nature's Path® Toaster Pastries (like Pop-Tarts® but no high-fructose corn syrup!)
12. '70s Mod orb lamps from White Trash in the East Village

Shopping 'til he drops with Goldy Lox, Design Wolf spots the perfect credenza upon which to place this spectacular lamp.

Food & Drink

Shrimp omelet with spicy cottage cheese

French press coffee, Cafe Bustelo® Espresso

Jonathan Adler® tableware on Orla Kiely® placemats

Macadamia Nut Liqueur + Pineapple OJ = MacNut Mimosa!

LIKES: Lean proteins, low carb deliciousness
DISLIKES: Red meat, except bacon and proscuitto (pink meat?)

NEW YORK CITY

BARS

1) The Eagle: 554 W 28th St • (646) 473-1886 • eaglenyc.com
2) Rockbar: 185 Christopher St • (212) 675-1864 • rockbarnyc.com
3) Ty's: 114 Christopher St • (212) 741-9641 • tysbarnyc.com

FOOD

4) The Breslin: 16 W 29th St • (212) 679-1939 • thebreslin.com
5) Elmo: 156 7th Ave • (212) 337-8000 • elmorestaurant.com
6) Sammy's Noodle Shop & Grill: 453 6th Ave • (212) 924-6688
7) The Shake Shack: Madison Square Park • (212) 889-6600 • shakeshack.com
8) Westville (East): 173 Ave A • (212) 677-2933 • westvillenyc.com

COFFEE

9) Billy's Bakery: 184 9th Ave • (212) 647-9956 • billysbakerynyc.com
10) Stumptown Coffee (Ace Hotel): 18 W 29th St • (347) 294-4295 • stumptowncoffee.com

FURNITURE

11) ABC Carpet and Home: 888 Broadway • (212) 473-3000 • abchome.com
12) Desiron: 151 Wooster St • (212) 353-2600 • desiron.com

SHOPPING

13) The End of History: 548 1/2 Hudson St #A • (212) 647-7598
theendofhistoryshop.blogspot.com
14) Klein Reid Studio: 51-02 21st St, 7th Floor, Long Island City • by appointment
(718) 937-3828 • kleinreid.com
15) Opening Ceremony (Ace Hotel): 1190 Broadway • (646) 695-5680 • aceopeningceremony.us
16) Rainbows and Triangles: 192 8th Ave #1 • (212) 627-2166 • rainbowsandtriangles.com

POINTS OF INTEREST

17) Fire Island Pines: Gaycation resort destination four miles off the Long Island coast
41 River Road, Sayville, NY • (631) 597-6500 • thepinesfireisland.com
18) The Highline: Public park built on a freight rail line elevated above Manhattan's West Side.
From Gansevoort St in the Meatpacking District to W 34th St between 10th and 11th Aves
(212) 500-6035 • thehighline.org
19) Madison Square Park: seven-acre urban oasis in the Flatiron District • E 23rd St
to E 26th St between Madison Ave and 5th Ave • madisonsquarepark.org
20) The Noguchi Museum: Displays the life's work of Japanese-American artist and designer
Isamu Noguchi • 9-01 33rd Rd, Long Island City • (718) 204-7088 • noguchi.org

MUSCLE BEAR

One of the most tantalizing creatures of the Bear world is Muscle Bear. A hybrid critter, he possesses traits similar to those of his muscled but hairless cousin, the Circuit Gay, while embracing his fur and keeping it au naturel. Grrrrr.

We find our particular Muscle Bear deep in the wilds of Silver Lake, a bohemian suburb on the east side of Los Angeles, largely populated by Alterna-Gays and straight-but-not-narrow, Creative Industry types. Here, he lives in close proximity to the studios—where he works as an assistant director—and to Silver Lake's Bear Central, a trifecta of neighborhood Bear bars: The Eagle, Faultline and Akbar.

Muscle Bear slumbers in an "Atomic Ranch," a style typical of the abodes built in this region during Hollywood's fabulous '50s. He has gone to painstaking lengths to authentically recreate the decade when restoring and decorating his "den." From researching classic color schemes in paints and tiles for his June Cleaver kitchen, to acquiring the perfect vintage pickup truck for his open-air carport, Muscle Bear is a perfectionist with an eye for detail.

He displays the same attention to detail with his delectable bod during his rigorous and regular workouts at Gold's Gym Hollywood and his cardio runs around Silver Lake Reservoir, both followed by consumption of Bear-quantities of protein and healthy snacks.

You can observe Muscle Bear scrounging for grub at the infamous Silver Lake Trader Joe's. While foraging for fresh broccoli and chicken breasts he observes the fascinating mating rituals of the local Bears, Otters and Wolves on the prowl for potential mates—as well as prosciutto and polenta!

When dining midday, Muscle Bear is often spotted at The Kitchen, a neighborhood favorite, where he splurges on succulent Buttermilk Fried Chicken Breasts, yummy Garlic Mashed Potatoes and fresh Succotash. For an afternoon pick-me-up, he likes to meet his production manager at the gorgeous LAMILL Coffee for a power shot of Espresso con Panna.

When entertaining clients, Muscle Bear delights in treating them to decadent, gourmet Italian meals at Osteria Mozza on Melrose, one of his guiltiest pleasures. Here, he devours the Whole Wheat Garganeli with Rabbit Ragout—all in the name of work, of course.

When he's not busy working on new commercials or working on his bod, Muscle Bear can be observed shopping in and around his own habitat. He especially adores vintage finds from the Mid-Century mercantile combo Amsterdam Modern - Mohawk General Store, and funky accessories from Yolk: Free Range Design. For more eye candy, he roams to Lawson-Fenning for a vintage, distressed-leather Barcelona chair and to ReForm School or Bar Keeper for groovy bar essentials. After all, he is creating the perfect Bear Lair.

Immersed in the cinematic history and culture of L.A., Muscle Bear often attends the nighttime, outdoor screenings of camp classics like *Cleopatra* at the Hollywood Forever Cemetery. Amazingly, this final resting place of so many Hollywood greats opens its gates at night for live concerts and movies projected onto the mausoleum wall. Muscle Bear pays his respects at Cecil B. DeMille's tomb before settling in on a lawn chair for the *Grease* sing-along.

Through his industry connections, Muscle Bear has an extended crew of friends in Palm Springs, a popular get-away for LA Bears. In fact, he and Tiki Bear are good friends and he has been known to crash at TB's swanky pad during high-profile Bear weekends. True to his name, Muscle Bear loves to challenge his physical endurance through adventurous ski trips to the Sierra Mountains. His most anticipated Bear weekend is with a certain Polar Bear for Elevation Mammoth Gay Ski Week where he hopes to share a cozy cabin with his rendezvous buddy.

Do you want the top or bottom bunk at Muscle Bear's sleepover?

> I enjoy playing "personal trainer" with a certain up and coming actor.

1. Gold's Gym® t-shirt – souvenir from an "extra" on Hawaiian film shoot
2. Apple iPod® Nano
3. Muscle Milk® protein shake (it's working!)
4. Banana from Trader Joe's® on Hyperion Ave (he walks; parking is horrendous)

5. Vintage hardware from Liz's Antique Hardware on La Brea Ave
6. Daltile® wall tiles from the Gallery showroom
7. Osterizer® blender for muscle-building, protein drinks (Bloody Marys on Sundays)
8. Eggs for protein smoothies
9. Whey powders for protein smoothies

Keeping his 1954 GMC 100 pickup in top shape with a good hose-down, Muscle bear takes "workin' at the carwash" to a new level of hotness.

Food & Drink

Muscle Milk® protein shake

Skinless chicken breast with broccoli

Melamine tableware and a placemat scored at "Tar-jay"

Toy truck (a gift from Polar Bear)

LIKES: Animal protein
DISLIKES: Soy protein

LOS ANGELES (SILVERLAKE)

BARS

1) Akbar: 4356 W Sunset Blvd • (323) 665-6810 • akbarsilverlake.com

2) The Eagle: 4219 Santa Monica Blvd • eaglela.com

3) Faultline Bar: 4216 Melrose Ave • (323) 660-0889 • faultlinebar.com

4) Tiki-Ti: 4427 Sunset Blvd • (323) 669-9381 • tiki-ti.com

FOOD

5) Alcove: 1929 Hillhurst Ave • (323) 644-0100 • alcovecafe.com

6) Cru: 1521 Griffith Park Blvd • (323) 667-1551 • crusilverlake.com

7) Elf: 2135 W Sunset Blvd • (213) 484-6829 • elfcafe.com

8) The Kitchen: 4348 Fountain Ave • (323) 664-3663 • thekitchen-silverlake.com

9) Osteria Mozza: 6602 Melrose Ave • (323) 297-0100 • osteriamozza.com

10) Phò Café: 2841 W Sunset Blvd • (213) 413-0888

11) Trader Joe's: 2730 Hyperion Ave • (323) 665-6774 • traderjoes.com

COFFEE

12) Intelligentsia Coffee & Tea: 3922 W Sunset Blvd • (323) 663-6173 • intelligentsiacoffee.com

13) LAMILL Coffee: 1636 Silver Lake Blvd • (323) 663-4441 • lamillcoffee.com

FURNITURE

14) Amsterdam Modern: 4011 W Sunset Blvd • (323) 669-1601 • amsterdammodern.com

15) Lawson-Fenning: 1618 Silver Lake Blvd • (323) 660-1500 • lawsonfenning.com

16) ReForm School: 3902 Sunset Blvd • (323) 906-8660 • reformschoolrules.com

17) Rubbish Interiors: 1627 Silver Lake Blvd • (323) 661-5575 • rubbishinteriors.com

18) Yolk: 1626 Silver Lake Blvd • (323) 660-4315 • shopyolk.com

SHOPPING

19) Bar Keeper: 3910 W Sunset Blvd • (323) 669-1675 • barkeepersilverlake.com

20) Mohawk General Store: 4011 W Sunset Blvd • (323) 669-1601 • mohawkgeneralstore.net

POINTS OF INTEREST

21) Gold's Gym: 1016 Cole Ave • (323) 462-7012 • goldsgym.com/hollywoodca

22) Hollywood Forever Cemetery: 6000 Santa Monica Blvd • (323) 469-1181 hollywoodforever.com

23) Silver Lake Reservoir: Open reservoirs supply water for South LA and recreation space for the people and dogs of Silver Lake • 1854-2246 Silver Lake Blvd • silverlakereservoirs.org

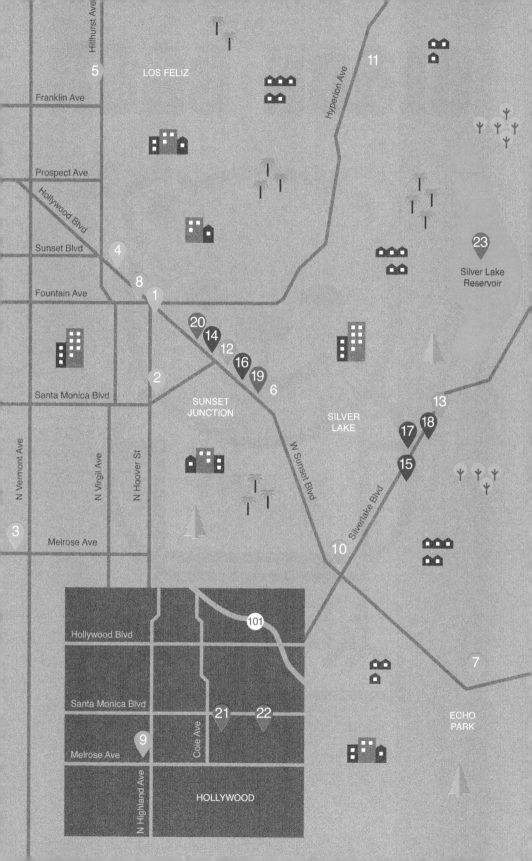

BLACK BEAR

Fun-loving, Philly-based Black Bear is known for his mercurial spirit and sexy swagger, evidenced by his devoted fan base amongst the inhabitants of the City of Brotherly Love. He is easy on the eyes and exudes tremendous confidence in his charmed career as the owner of a popular comic book shop in the center of Old City Philadelphia. Because his passion is also his work, he spends much of his time at the store, entertaining friends and customers with his raucous humor and seemingly infinite knowledge of super hero trivia.

It's no accident that Black Bear followed this line of work; he was devouring comic books at the age of five. He once read "Batman: The Killing Joke," cover-to-cover in Japanese—quite a feat for a non-Japanese-speaking Philly boy.

His favorite superhero has always been the Green Lantern. Like that emerald-hued avenger, Black Bear is fueled by his strong will, his passion for justice, and the thrill of "fighting for the little guy." He cleverly named his comic book shop The 'Zine Lantern as an homage to the character who has inspired him to actively participate on his local business council and in various neighborhood improvement groups.

Black Bear makes his home in the "Gayborhood" of Center City in a brownstone packed to the rafters with collections of vintage comics, robot toys, and Japanese ephemera. Acknowledging that he does not posses any interior design superpowers, he makes the latest electronic gadgets the centerpieces of his comfortable dude den.

Black Bear is a devoted student of the martial arts, keeping his form and mind sharp with daily training at the Zhang Sah Martial Arts studio. He is frequently spotted perfecting his bodacious bod through rigorous weight training at 12th Street Gym.

On weekends, BB visits Giovanni's Room on 12th Street, one of the oldest gay bookstores in the country. You can easily observe him here as he immerses himself in the latest science fiction and fantasy novels. He also saunters through the vintage stores along South Street, always on the lookout for the elusive vintage comic or authentic 1950s tin robot.

A typical Philly boy, he is loyal to his favorite hoagie shop, Cosmi's Deli, where he devours the Cheesesteak Trio with a local Summer Love Ale. For a quick feeding, Black Bear runs to The Continental for a zesty lunch of Thai Chicken Skewers. Weekday mornings, before he opens his shop, he might dash to the Reading Terminal Market for some lunch fixin's. "Ka-pow!" he snatches the last heirloom tomato for the tasty sandwiches he'll make for his employees. His stealth and ninja-tastic moves, coupled with his charm, are the double whammy he needs to navigate Philly's historic farmers' market with aplomb.

Black Bear is quite the charmer and considered a veritable Bear's Bear. He can be seen at Westbury or Woody's, showing off his dance moves and flashing his enigmatic smile with the latest Bear Du Jour in tow. Once a month, he haunts Kickstand Philly, a Saturday night Bear party held at The Bike Stop, Philly's mecca of Levi's and leather. It is at these eclectic watering holes that Black Bear likes to strike a superhero pose and display his mighty, muscular body.

Even superheroes need a break now and again. For relaxing escapes, Black Bear breaks out his green, 1960 Plymouth Fury convertible, rounds up his buds, and high tails it up to New Hope, PA. There, the furry beasts can be seen lounging by the pool at The Raven Resort while cooling down with margaritas from the cabana bar and enjoying the scenery. BB also loves driving to Asbury Park, NJ to soak up the sun and play in the surf with the other Bears. Some lucky devil always gets to ride shotgun.

Do you want to play Black Bear's superhero side-kick?

You'll have to buy me a drink to discover my super power.

1. High-res graphics monitor for designing his own comic book
2. Guinness® Stout
3. Paintings and screen prints he made in college
4. Collection of thrift store robots
5. Vintage comic books
6. Wacom® graphics tablet
7. Miigii, Dunny®, and Domo®!
8. T-shirt from Urban Outfitters® on Walnut St
9. Black SKECHERS® tennies

Kicking it in his Dojo, Black Bear practices his karate moves in case he has to protect Philly from a crazy octopus man or some other bad guy!

Food & Drink

Philly cheesesteak with sweet peppers and fries

Wheatgrass juice in Captain America® shot glass

Guinness® stout in Green Lantern® tumbler

Tastykake® Butterscotch Krimpets, guarded by Domo®

LIKES: Movie popcorn and Tang®
DISLIKES: Tofu, Tofurky®, and Tofutti®

PHILADELPHIA

BARS

1) The Bike Stop: 206 S Quince St • (215) 627-1662 • thebikestop.com
2) Westbury: 261 S 13th St • (215) 546-5170 • westburybarandrestaurant.com
3) Woody's: 202 S 13th St • (215) 545-1893 • woodysbar.com

FOOD

4) The Continental: 138 Market St • (215) 923-6069 • continentalmartinibar.com
5) Cosmi's Deli: 1501 S 8th St • (215) 468-6093 • cosmideli.com
6) More Than Just Ice Cream: 1119 Locust St • (215) 574-0586 • morethanjusticecream.com
7) Reading Terminal Market: 51 N 12th St • (215) 922-2317 • readingterminalmarket.org

COFFEE

8) One Shot Coffee: 217 W George St • (215) 627-1620 • 1shotcoffee.com
9) Philadelphia Java Company: from *It's Always Sunny in Philadelphia* • 518 S 4th S
   (215) 928-1811

FURNITURE

10) Hello Home: 1004 Pine St • (215) 545-7060 • shophelloworld.com
11) Mode Moderne: 159 N 3rd St • (215) 627-0299 • modemoderne.com

SHOPPING

12) Astro Vintage: 720 S 5th St • (215) 922-0483 • astrovintage.com
13) Brave New Worlds: 45 N 2nd St • (215) 925-6525 • bravenewworldscomics.com
14) Giovanni's Room: 345 S 12th St • (215) 923-2960 • queerbooks.com
15) Retrospect Vintage: 508 South St • (267) 671-0116 • retrospectvintage.com
16) Urban Outfitters: 1627 Walnut St • (215) 569-3131 • urbanoutfitters.com

POINTS OF INTEREST

17) 12th St Gym: 204 S 12th St • (215) 985-4092 • 12streetgym.com
18) Zhang Sah Martial Arts: 530 Bainbridge St • (215) 923-6676 • zhangsah.org
19) The Raven Resort: 385 West Bridge St, New Hope, PA • (215) 862-2081
    theravennewhope.com
20) 5th Avenue (Gay) Beach: 1300 Ocean Ave (just south of Convention Hall), Asbury Park NJ
21) The Liberty Bell Center: Houses the freakin' Liberty Bell! • 526 Market St • (215) 965-2305
    nps.gov/inde/liberty-bell-center.htm

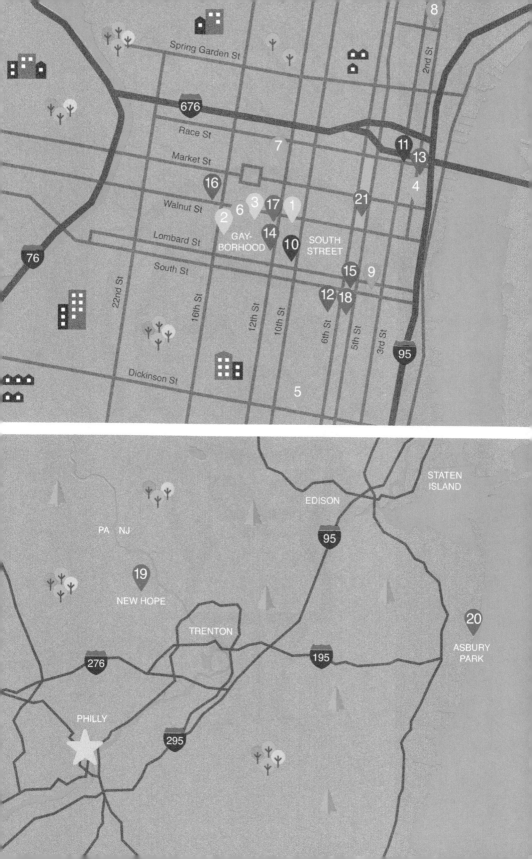

Goldy Lox

Gorgeous Goldy Lox is a rare creature indeed. Her personal ecosystem is lovingly defined by the Bears and Wolves she adores. Although she possesses stunning looks and a sparkling personality, she cautiously avoids mating entanglements with the males of her species. By selectively socializing with her Bear "boys," she escapes the unwanted pawing of the breeder scene.

Goldy thrives in fashion-obsessed Miami, the land of beautiful people. She can be spotted at her design desk thoughtfully sketching sunny, resort-inspired polo shirts and club ensembles for hipster Gays. The flattering, tropical shirts that she custom designs for her stocky Bear buddies have made her a local fashion favorite. Her latest obsession is the TexShow at the Javitz Center in NYC where she hooks up with Design Wolf—her mentor, model and muse—to hunt through a goldmine of original, designer fabrics. Goldy Lox's ultimate goal is to be the first famous, female designer for men.

On any given day, you can find Goldy nesting in her high-glam, live/work loft in the Wynwood Arts District, where she rents from Design Wolf. She adores her all-white bachelorette pad, glamorously styled with white, button-tufted leather sofas, enormous Regency mirrors, and white, fur rugs on glossy, espresso-colored floors.

Design Wolf relishes his frequent migrations from NYC to FL where he pals around with Goldy and plays in the sun with the toned and tanned beach Bears. When Goldy and DW are feeling frisky, they journey up the coastline to Fort Lauderdale to treasure shop and bar hop. Their favorite trek starts with a stop at Bill's Filling Station, followed by a tropical cocktail at Mai-Kai before Design Wolf breaks away for a night at the Ramrod. Occasionally, they call it an early evening so they can start their morning hunt bright-eyed and bushy-tailed. But if they've been wild, nocturnal animals, they usually stop in to Peter Pan Diner in Oakland Park for an "early breakfast" by the light of the moon. Once Goldy and Wolf shake off the night, they hit estate sales, scouting for a bargain Tommi Parzinger lamp, or Goldy's personal passion—antique perfume bottles.

When Goldy is craving a little porridge, Design Wolf likes treating her to fashionable lunches at Michael's Genuine Food & Drink in the Miami Design District. You may catch a glimpse of them devouring the Deviled Eggs and Florida Rock Shrimp Salad and imbibing Strawberry-Basil Caipirinhas.

On rare occasions, Goldy indulges her urge to peruse "potential ex-husbands," as she jokingly calls them. She drags Design Wolf to the Blue Martini Lounge on South Miami Avenue for a little taste of the chase, but they inevitably end up dancing the night away with the boys at Twist in South Beach.

Goldy's strict Sunday ritual begins with a morning of tennis at the Flamingo Park courts followed by post-lunch "errands" on Lincoln Road. Her list may include popping into the ultra hip boutique, Base, for travel accessories, a new dance record, or UrbanEars headphones. She often makes a quick stop at Fly Boutique to peruse the men's fashions for some vintage design inspiration. Later she catches some afternoon rays, tanning at the 12th Street Gay Beach. The fun and sun lead up to Sunday Tea at Palace, where Wolf joins her after his workout at the David Barton gym.

When Goldy feels particularly mischievous, she grabs Design Wolf for a work/play excursion to Fort Lauderdale—where the Bears are. With her arm around her guardian Wolf, she counts her blessings that she was not born a Little Red Riding Hood. Goldy Lox's innocent charm and authentic sweetness completely endear her to the Bears of Miami and Fort Lauderdale. On these outings, she seems to always meet new clients and get her cocktails for free.

Who's the Goldy Lox in your Bear crew?

I like my bed soft, my porridge hot, and my men... just right.

1. Dream Board
2. Fire Island party flyer from last summer with Design Wolf
3. Trina Turk® store card from Bal Harbor boutique
4. Apple Macbook® with pink Marc Jacobs® sleeve
5. Vintage fabrics (to make ascots for Wolf and Bear friends)
6. Christian Dior® slingback heels
7. Ted Baker® shift dress from the Cocowalk "lifestyle center"
8. Pink ribbon belt designed by Goldy herself
9. Martini and Rossi® Asti mini
10. Apple iPhone® (white, of course)
11. Vintage, male dress form
12. Sleek, clear, acrylic mannequin

Perfecting her stylish serve, Goldy Lox never misses her weekly tennis date in Flamingo Park – sensible shoes optional!

Food & Drink

Whole Foods® steel cut oatmeal with fresh red berries

Cucumber DRY® soda, on the rocks

Missoni® for Target® bowl on preppy placemat

Enamelware jigger with exactly 1oz shot of cream

LIKES: Generous, fluffy salads
DISLIKES: Red food dye - she's allergic

MIAMI / FT LAUDERDALE

BARS

1) Bills Filling Station: 2209 Wilton Dr, Wilton Manors • (954) 567-5978 • billsfillingstation.com
2) Cubby Hole: 823 N Federal Hwy, Fort Lauderdale • (954) 728-9001 • thecubbyhole.com
3) Palace Bar: 1200 Ocean Dr, Miami Beach • (305) 531-7234 • palacesouthbeach.com
4) Ramrod Bar: 1508 NE 4th Ave, Fort Lauderdale • (954) 763-8219 • ramrodbar.com
5) Twist: 1057 Washington Ave, Miami Beach • (305) 538-9478 • twistsobe.com

FOOD

6) Balans: 1022 Lincoln Rd, Miami Beach • (305) 534-9191 • balansrestaurants.com
7) Don Arturo's: 1198 SW 27th Ave, Fort Lauderdale • (954) 584-7966
8) Mai-Kai: 3599 N Federal Hwy, Fort Lauderdale • (954) 563-3272 • maikai.com
9) Michael's Genuine Food & Drink: Atlas Plaza, 130 NE 40th St • (305) 573-5550 michaelsgenuine.com
10) Peter Pan Diner: 1216 E Oakland Park Blvd, Oakland Park • (954) 565-7177
11) Rosie's Bar & Grill: 2449 Wilton Dr, Wilton Manors • (954) 567-1320 • rosiesbarandgrill.com

COFFEE

12) David's Cafe: 1058 Collins Ave, Miami Beach • (305) 534-8736 • davidscafe.com
13) Panther Coffee: 2390 NW 2nd Ave • (305) 677-3952 • panthercoffee.com
14) Starbucks: "Bearbucks" 1015 NE 26th St, Wilton Manors • (954) 566-1304 starbucks.com/store/17302

FURNITURE

15) Senzatempo: 1655 Meridian Ave, Miami Beach • (305) 534-5588 • senzatempo.com
16) Shades of the Past: 2360 Wilton Dr, Wilton Manors • (954) 829-3726
17) Space Modern: 2335 NE 26th St, Fort Lauderdale • (954) 564-6100 • space-modern.com

SHOPPING

18) Base: 939 Lincoln Rd, South Beach • (305) 531-4982 • baseworld.com
19) Leather Werks: 1226 NE 4th Ave, Fort Lauderdale • (954) 761-1236 • leatherwerks.com
20) Fly Boutique: • 650 Lincoln Rd, Miami Beach • (305) 604-8508

POINTS OF INTEREST

21) Art Deco Welcome Center: 1001 Ocean Dr, Miami Beach • (305) 763-8026 artdecowelcomecenter.com
22) David Barton Gym: 2323 Collins Ave, Miami Beach • (305) 534-1660 • davidbartongym.com
23) Flamingo Park: 11th St and Jefferson Ave, Miami Beach • (305) 673-7766 miamibeachparks.com
24) Coconut Grove Organic Farmer's Market: Saturdays, 3300 Grand Ave • (305) 238-7747 glaserorganicfarms.com

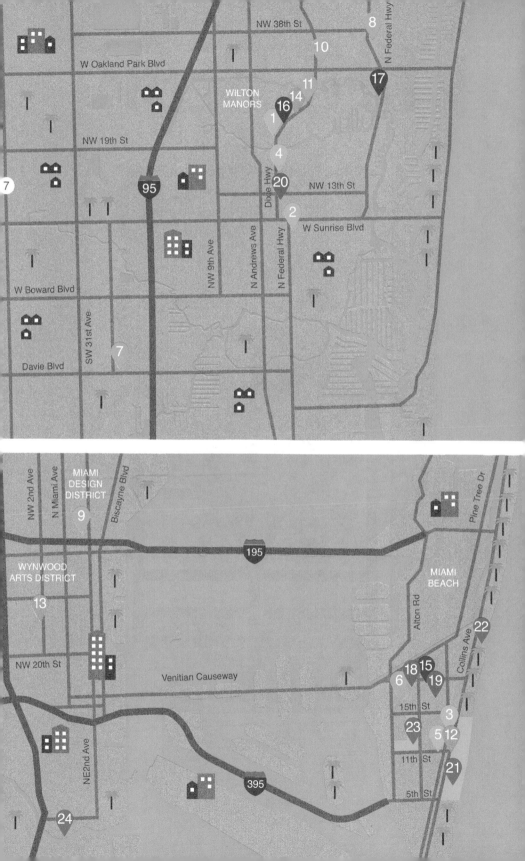

TiKi BEAR

Tiki Bears originally evolved on the volcanic islands of the Southern Pacific, but these sexy, coco-skinned specimens often migrate from Polynesia to the mainland to the delight of many-a-Bear. Our lava-hot Bear has trekked from the tropical oasis of Hawaii to the Mid-Century design oasis of Palm Springs, CA—a happening haven for fun-loving, sun-loving creatures.

Among the palm-lined lanes of Palm Springs, our gregarious Tiki Bear has carved a life of adventure and leisure from his successful career in Mid-Century Modern real estate. He dedicates ample time to his favorite pursuits; namely, Mid-Century architecture and Tikiana. One of Tiki Bear's favorite pastimes is hosting fabulous fundraising events at his Tiki-themed, Alexander-designed home in the iconic Twin Palms neighborhood. Many of his famously fun parties support the Palm Springs Modern Committee, a non-profit dedicated to the heritage of modern architecture, like Tiki Bear's own lair.

A lively and social creature, Tiki Bear is regularly spotted at art galleries downtown or at the Palm Springs Art Museum, often with a visiting Modern Bear on his arm. Together, they certainly make a handsome Bearnamic Duo.

Tiki Bear is more of a collector than a consumer, but he will gladly engage in some boutiquing with Modern Bear, shopping for sexy, designer shirts at Wil Stiles and party-ready, patterned slacks from Mr. Turk. At Trina Turk Residential they find ultra-hip baraphernalia and, next door, Mid-Century inspired planters and lighting at Just Modern. When hunting for authentic, vintage Tiki accoutrements for his Bear Lair, TB beats a path to the hip, retro store, Dazzles. If he's feeling lucky, Tiki Bear rounds the Palm Canyon curve to scour the tucked-away shops of Perez Road in Cathedral City.

TB's feeding habits are more like personal rituals. He tames his hungry beast with daily breakfasts at Manhattan In the Desert on East Palm Canyon and Bear-sized lunches at John's Restaurant north of downtown. When he's feeling "fancy," Tiki Bear treats himself, and the oft-visiting Modern Bear, to scrumptious dinners of Roasted Rack of Lamb at Lulu California Bistro or Crawfish Pot Pie at Trio.

On occasion, Tiki Bear ventures into the local wilds for an evening of fun. He prefers Hunters when he's feeling a bit tame and Tool Shed when his animal instincts are up for some prowling. On Wednesday nights, he goes cruising—in his 1962 Thunderbird—after hosting a party with the local G.A.Y. (Great Automobiles of Yesteryear) appreciation club.

When the desert climate is mild, TB loves hiking in Taquitz Canyon, or sometimes deep in Mecca Hills where you might find him au naturel, an experience that is surprisingly common in the more discreet mountain areas of Palm Springs. On gorgeous winter days, our charming Bear is known to lead his pack of friends or clients up the mountainside to reveal a breathtaking view of his beloved desert paradise.

Saturday mornings, when he isn't showing a Mid-Century gem to potential buyers, Tiki Bear can be found relaxing and drinking lattes with his Bear buddies in the courtyard behind Koffi on North Palm Canyon Drive. Sunday afternoons are ceremoniously devoted to "Bear" Bust at The Barracks, just down the road in "Cat City." TB dreams of opening an authentic Tiki bar in Palm Springs, like the famous party spots of Hollywood's heyday. In preparation, he treats visiting house guests and partygoers to elaborately-garnished tropical drinks, swinging nights of exotica lounge music (Martin Denny LP's!) on his Magnavox turntable, and sometimes a wild bongo solo!

Would you like to Mai-Tai one on with Tiki Bear?

Greg and Bobby told me this Tiki idol was bad luck, but my Palm Springs paradise begs to differ.

1. Realtor Supra® Key
2. '50s Rattan bar
3. Mai Tai, Trader Vic's® recipe
4. Cocktail garnishes
5. '70s Suspended ashtray (now a birdhouse!)

6. Oranges from his own tree
7. Freshly cut pineapple from his neighbor's tree
8. Tropical shirt by Shag®
9. Requisite Tiki torches
10. '60s patio saucer chairs from Swank Interiors

Debating "how to stuff a wild mankini" with his party guests, Tiki Bear slaps out some "Yellow Bird" by Arthur Lyman on his trusty bongos.

Food & Drink

Firecracker shrimp over fried rice

Spicy California roll with wasabi and ginger

Fresh, tropical mango

Longboard Lager®

Vintage Tiki table setting

LIKES: Anything hot-n-spicy with a cold beer
DISLIKES: Alfalfa sprouts

PALM SPRINGS

BARS

1) The Amigo Room (Ace Hotel): 701 E Palm Canyon Dr • (760) 325-9900 • acehotel.com
2) Barracks: 67-625 E Palm Canyon Dr, Cathedral City • (760) 321-9688 • thebarracksbarps.com
3) Hunters: 302 E Arenas Rd • (760) 323-0700 • huntersnightclubs.com
4) Street Bar: 224 E Arenas Rd • (760) 320-1266 • psstreetbar.com
5) Tool Shed: 600 Sunny Dunes Rd • (760) 320-3299 • toolshed-ps.com

FOOD

6) El Jefe (Saguaro Hotel): 1800 E Palm Canyon Dr • (760) 323-1711
7) Jaio: 515 N Palm Canyon Dr • (760) 321-1424
8) John's: 900 N Palm Canyon Dr • (760) 327-8522
9) Trio: 707 N Palm Canyon Dr • (760) 864-8746 • triopalmsprings.com

COFFEE

10) Koffi: The Corridor • 515 N Palm Canyon Dr • kofficoffee.com

FURNITURE

11) A La Mod: 844 N Palm Canyon Dr • 760-327-0707 • alamod768.com
12) Dazzles: 1035 N Palm Canyon Dr • (760) 327-1446
13) Flow Modern Design: 768 N Palm Canyon Dr • (760) 322-0768 • flowmoderndesign.com
14) Just Modern: 901 N Palm Canyon Dr • (760) 322-5600 • justmoderndecor.com
15) Modernway: 745 N Palm Canyon Dr • (760) 320-5455 • psmodernway.com
16) Perez Road Shops: 68929 Perez Rd, Cathedral City •
    At HOM: (760) 770-4447 • at-hom.com
    Hedge: (760) 770-0090 • hedgepalmsprings.com
    JP Denmark: (760) 408-9147 • jpantik.com
    Spaces: (760) 770-5333 • modern-spaces.net

SHOPPING

17) Raymond/Lawrence: 830 N Palm Canyon Dr • (760) 322-3344 • raymond-lawrence.com
18) Shag Store: 725 N Palm Canyon Dr • (760) 322-3400 • shagstore.com
19) Trina Turk – Mr. Turk – Trina Turk Residential: 891 N Palm Canyon Dr • (760) 416-2856
    trinaturk.com
20) Wil Stiles: 875 N Palm Canyon Dr • (760) 327-9764 • wilstiles.com

POINTS OF INTEREST

21) Ace Hotel & Swim Club: Renovated mid-century modern motel with a party pool, King's
    Highway diner, and Amigo Room bar • 701 E Palm Canyon Dr • acehotel.com
22) Caliente Tropics: '60s Tiki and Polynesian styled hotel • 411 E Palm Canyon Dr
    (760) 327-1391• calientetropics.com
23) The Parker Meridien: Norma's five-star diner • 4200 E Palm Canyon Dr • (760) 770-5000
24) Palm Springs Art Museum • 101 N Museum Dr • 760-322-4800 • psmuseum.org

PANDA BEAR

Our smart and savvy Panda Bear is one of the more unusual creatures in the Bear world as he leads a unique, dual existence in Seattle, WA. By day, the former curator of the Seattle Asian Art Museum is a successful and serious gallery owner. At night, he transforms into an ultra-hip DJ spinning at clubs in the Emerald City and across the border in Vancouver, BC. These seemingly different pursuits reveal his innate talent for discovering emerging artists.

Panda Bear makes his habitat in a loft located in a 1930s Art Deco building in the "Gayborhood" of Capitol Hill. Decorated in Minimalist Asian Modern, his private sanctuary showcases his favorite art pieces—the ones he affectionately refers to as his "keepers." In his cleverly camouflaged, home music studio, Panda Bear creates new podcasts and fine-tunes the playlists he debuts at clubs on the weekends. His dual mixing boards and many tech toys hide in a Shandong trunk chest that has been in his family for over two centuries. Other key pieces in PB's domicile have been carefully culled from his favorite furniture shop, Chidori Asian Antiques.

Panda Bear strives for the perfect mix on the dance floor AND in his art gallery where he carefully curates an eclectic and exciting visual experience. Weekly foraging visits to Everyday Music in Capitol Hill edify his music collection. Weekly meetings with visual artists throughout the Pacific Northwest round out his talent stable. His gallery proudly promotes local artists and Native American culture while pushing the avant-garde envelope. One of his artists makes painstakingly-researched, modern totem poles that Bill and Melinda Gates are wild about.

When Panda Bear has a free evening and is feeling amorous, he traipses to C.C. Attle's on Capitol Hill or Diesel in the Central District to track down a delicious Daddy Bear. He also enjoys meeting up with his pals at The Cuff for Bear-aoke on Tuesdays where he performs a stellar rendition of Stevie Nicks' "Stand Back."

For a truly guilty pleasure, PB and his buds migrate to the über-kitsch Unicorn Club to indulge in their signature cocktail, Unicorn Jizz, and Crispy Fried Exploding Twinkies.

The sole vegetarian of the bear species, Panda Bear regularly satiates his ferocious appetite by devouring a Buffalo Portobello Mushroom Burger at Plum Bistro on 12th Avenue or munching on Vietnamese comfort food at Phó Cyclo Café on Broadway. Soup is good food, especially during Seattle's notorious rainy season when you may find our Panda steaming up his glasses while sharing a piping hot bowl of Phó with a handsome, hungry Bear.

Seattleites adore their coffee and Panda Bear is no exception. He hunts down his daily brew from local darling Peet's Coffee & Tea or People's Republic of Koffee, where java isn't the only hot and steamy item on the menu. Look closely and you may see a dribble of melted cheese in his whiskers from their delectably creamy Grilled Cheese Sandwich complimented with a cup of Tomato Soup.

To satisfy his fashion cravings, PB loves Kuhlman in Belltown, where he treats himself to J. Lindeberg button-down shirts, dark denim Nudie Jeans and an occasional Nixon watch. For special dates with a Daddy Bear, our Panda submits to his darker half and heads to Pike Street to shop for toys at Babeland and Doghouse Leathers.

Panda Bear DJ's up and down the Pacific Northwest, often at Bear clubs like Pumpjack Pub and Numbers Cabaret in Vancouver, Canada. In his home environment, he can be found commanding the DJ booth and the dance floor at Neighbours and the Eagle. He religiously begins each night with Elastica's "Connection." You see, Panda Bear is a hopeless romantic who envisions furry, dancing men finding their soul mates during his performances.

Are you ready for a spin with Panda Bear?

I have loose standards when it comes to art and culture. Just call me "culture slut.

1. WeSC® DJ Aoki Pro headphones
2. Midi dual turntable deck (opposite page)
3) Peet's Coffee® Caffé Americano
4. Cotton t-shirt from Banana Republic® flagship store
5. No shoes in the house, please
6. Margo Selski painting, "Held (Memory II)" 2007, oil and beeswax on canvas
7. Civilianaire® denim from Ian on 2nd Ave
8. SIFF (Seattle International Film Festival) tickets in back pocket
9. Odd Nerdrum monograph
10. Ching Dynasty console (seriously Vintage!) from Chidori Asian Antiques
11. Rigaud® pine oil candle from The Beauty Bar

Spinning after another successful art opening at his gallery, Panda Bear gets the crowd riled up with a clever mix of Brit-pop singles and alterna-club hits.

Food & Drink

Veggie Phó
(Vietnamese noodle soup)

Shrimp spring roll with peanut sauce

Oolong tea in Bodum® mug from Blackbird in Ballard

Enamelware cherry blossom plate from Kiln Design

LIKES: The term "Flexitarian"
DISLIKES: Fois Gras

SEATTLE

BARS

1) C.C. Attle's: 1701 E Olive Way • (206) 726-0565 • ccattles.net
2) The Cuff: Tuesday Bearaoke • 1533 13th Ave • (206) 323-1525 • cuffcomplex.com
3) The Eagle: 314 E Pike St • (206) 621-7591 • seattleeagle.com
4) Diesel: 1413 14th Ave • (206) 322-1080 • dieselseattle.com
5) Neighbours: 1509 Broadway • (206) 324-5358 • neighboursnightclub.com
6) Numbers Cabaret: 1042 Davie Street, Vancouver BC • +1(604) 685-4077 • numbers.ca
7) Pumpjack Pub: 1167 Davie St, Vancouver BC • +1(604) 685-3417 • pumpjackpub.com

FOOD

8) Phó Cyclo Café: 406 Broadway Ave E • (206) 329-9256 • phocylcocafe.com
9) Plum Bistro: 1429 12th Ave • (206) 838-5333 • plumbistro.com
10) Unicorn: 1118 E Pike Street • (206) 325-6492 • unicornseattle.com

COFFEE

11) Caffé Vita: 1005 E Pike St • (206) 709-4440 • caffevita.com
12) Kaladi Brothers Coffee: 511 E Pike St • (206) 388-1700 • kaladi.com
13) People's Republic of Koffee: 1718 12th Ave • (206) 755-5727
14) Peet's Coffee: 1833 Broadway • (206) 438-8300 • peets.com

FURNITURE

15) Area 51: 401 E Pine St • (206) 568-4782 • area51seattle.com
16) Chartreuse: 2609 1st Ave • (206) 328-4844 • modchartreuse.com
17) Chidori Asian Antiques: 108 S Jackson St • (206) 343-7736 • chidoriantiques.com
18) Retrofit Home: 1103 E Pike St • (206) 568-4663 • retrofithome.com

SHOPPING

19) Babeland: 707 E Pike St • (206) 328-2914 • babeland.com/seattle
20) Dog House Leather: 1312 E Pike St • (206) 257-0231 • doghouseleathers.com
21) Everyday Music: 1520 10th Ave • (206) 568-3321 • everydaymusic.com
22) Kuhlman: 2419 1st Ave • (206) 441-1999 • kuhlmanseattle.com

POINTS OF INTEREST

23) Seattle Asian Art Museum: 1400 E Prospect • (206) 625-8900 • seattleartmuseum.org
24) Seattle Art Museum: 1300 First Ave • (206) 654-3100 • seattleartmuseum.org
25) Eastlake: Neighborhood with Modernist architecture and a visually impressive, permanent, water community of multi-story houseboats!

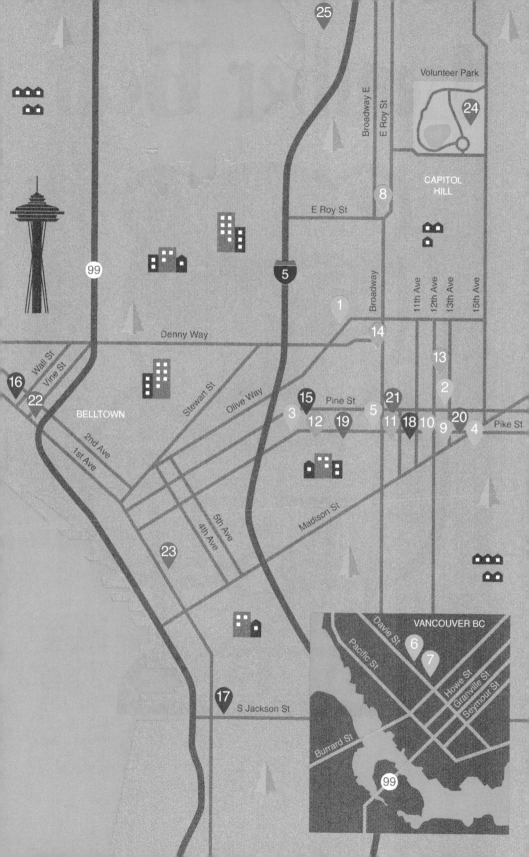

Leather Bear

Seductive and mysterious, the nocturnal Leather Bear is an especially captivating member of the Bear family. His proclivity for the leather world provides a welcome escape from his daytime persona as a criminal attorney.

We chanced upon this handsome Leather Bear in his natural habitat, a posh townhouse in Midtown Atlanta decorated with a sophisticated collection of chrome and white leather furnishings. But this den of glamorous Hollywood Regency décor belies Leather Bear's decadently dark alter ego.

Leather Bear treasures the finest things in life, like a perfectly hand-rolled Cuban cigar (he loves to be called "Cigar Daddy"), a smooth 30-year cognac, and a top-of-the-line leather sling for his "rec room."

He enjoys taking his friends on antique-hunting excursions where he shows off his taste for a style he jovially calls "Rococo-A-Go-Go"—sexy, over-the-top glitz and glamour. LB's favorite hunting grounds include the highbrow showroom, Belvedere, in Northside and the eclectic boutique, Paris on Ponce. When traveling solo, he frequently saunters in to the Eagle's basement, a specialty store where he finds new leather accessories and "toys" for his ever-growing collection.

In the daytime, Leather Bear dons his "Lawyer Drag" of a suit and tie, commanding considerable respect in the courtroom from his professional peers. He adds a bit of flair to his look with dress shirts and pocket squares from Sid Mashburn. At night, he commands respect in quite a different outfit. A leather harness to accentuate his hot, hairy chest thrills him as much as a pair of distressed leather Copenhagen chairs from his local Restoration Hardware.

When the mood to flaunt his leathers strikes this Bear, he cruises over to The Heretic on Friday nights and Eagle Atlanta on Saturdays. You can also find him mingling at the notoriously "hot and sticky" Manshaft parties at Cockpit. It is at these popular Bear watering holes where our specimen thrives, cutting a sexy figure in skin-tight chaps and vest. You see, Leather Bear Tops are prized in these dens and he comes prepared to please.

Leather Bear's beckoning eyes and flirtatious smirk will entice you back to his swanky Playbear Pad. His paramours are never disappointed. LB willingly takes the opportunity to employ those "borrowed" handcuffs from the courthouse, much to the delight of his overnight playmates. For adventures away from home, LB heads to Chicago each spring for International Mr. Leather where he romps with other Leather Bears from around the globe.

Weekend days bring out the lighter side of Leather Bear. You can frequently observe him enjoying such wholesome activities as playing softball in Piedmont Park and socializing at "Bearbucks" in Ansley Mall. An occasional outing to Woof's sports bar on Piedmont for happy hour rounds out his weekend fun.

Leather Bear's feeding habits are quite varied and include everything from Nutella & Burnt Marshmallow shakes from Flip Burger Boutique to decadent Southern cooking at award-winning Watershed. Serious caffeine cravings are sated at the renowned Octane Coffee on Marietta Street. He loves to satisfy his protein cravings at Roxx, feasting on the Aged Filet Steak with Whipped Potatoes and Green Beans. He burns off all of these indulgences with dedicated workouts at Urban Body Fitness.

LB's beloved mode of transportation is his "prestigious" black convertible Mercedes SL Roadster. He also loves day trips to Athens, GA on his pride and joy—a red, vintage, 1966 Honda Dream 305. His excellent eye for design appreciates the contrast of his black leathers against the flawless, red motorbike. When the weather is right, he hits the road for long weekends with the Gay motorcycle club, LOSTBOYS. With the wind in his face and some "sticks" in his vest pocket, Leather Bear is ready for excitement and adventure.

Are you man enough to ride "bitch" with Leather Bear?

You can never have enough lucite, leather, or sex toys!

1. La Gloria Cubana® Serie R cigar
2. Dunhill® crystal cigar ashtray
3. '50s bar cart with vintage decanters
4. Leather chaps and shirt from the Eagle
5. SafeTGuard® jockstrap
6. Brahma® Bruiser boots

7. Samsung® smartphone
8. '60s mirrored credenza from Belvedere
9. Hollywood Regency lamps by Reclaimed Light
10. Strangely sexy Stallion painting from Paris on Ponce
11. Courvoisier® XO Imperial Cognac

Cruising downtown on his sexy motorbike, Leather Bear prepares himself for an important "de-briefing" at The Cockpit.

Food & Drink

Filet Mignon, rare

Classic baked potato with all the fixin's

French green beans

Wild berry blossom pastry

2008 Pulenta Estate Gran Malbec

LIKES: Grass fed beef
DISLIKES: Fusion cuisine; K.I.S.S.!

ATLANTA

BARS

1) The Cockpit: Manshaft Party • 465 Boulevard SE • (404) 343-2450
   the cockpit-atlanta.blogspot.com
2) The Eagle: 306 Ponce De Leon Ave • (404) 873-2453 • atlantaeagle.com
3) The Heretic: 2069 Chesire Bridge Rd NE • (404) 325-3061 • hereticatlanta.com
4) Woof's: 2425 Piedmont Rd NE • (404) 869-9422 • woofsatlanta.com

FOOD

5) Flip Burger Boutique : 1587 Howell Mill Rd • (404) 352-3547 • flipburgerboutique.com
6) Fox Brother's Bar-B-Q: 1238 Dekalb Ave NE • (404) 577-4030 • foxbrosbbq.com
7) Roxx Tavern: 1824 Cheshire Bridge Rd NE • (404) 892-4541
8) Watershed: 1820 Peachtree Rd NW • (404) 809-3561 • watershedrestaurant.com

COFFEE

9) Aurora Coffee: 468 Moreland Ave NE • (404) 523-6856 • auroracoffee.com
10) Octane Coffee: 1009-B Marietta St NW • (404) 815-9886 • octanecoffee.com
11) Starbucks Ansley Mall: "Bearbucks" • 1544 Piedmont Rd NE • (404) 876-0629
    starbucks.com/store/14958

FURNITURE

12) Belvedere: 721 Miami Circle NE #105 • (404) 352-1942 • belvedereinc.com
13) City Issue: 325 Elizabeth St NE • (678) 999-9075 • cityissue.com
14) Paris on Ponce: 716 Ponce De Leon Place NE • (404) 249-9965 • parisonponce.com

SHOPPING

15) Rawhide Leather (The Eagle): 306 Ponce De Leon Ave NE • (404) 881-0031
16) Sid Mashburn: 1198 Howell Mill Rd NW • (404) 350-7135 • sidmashburn.com
17) Wish: 447 Moreland Ave NE • (404) 880-0402 • wishatl.com

POINTS OF INTEREST

18) Ansley Park: Affluent Midtown neighborhood considered the most gay-family-friendly
    in Atlanta.
19) Atlanta Botanical Garden: 1345 Piedmont Ave NE • (404) 876-5859 •
    atlantabotanicalgarden.org
20) Piedmont Park: Midtown park with playing fields, dog parks, running trails, and an
    amphitheater featuring national acts • 1320 Monroe Dr NE • piedmontpark.org
21) Urban Body Fitness: 500 Amsterdam Ave • (404) 885-1499 • urbanbodyfitness.com

HOTTER OTTER

A breed unto himself, the furry, but svelte, Hotter Otter makes quite a splash in the Bear Family. Both critters exhibit good-natured and fun-loving personalities that play well together. Exceedingly intelligent and creative, Hotter Otter loves to indulge his endearing playfulness at the many different Bear Runs across the country.

His environment of choice is a live/work loft in the Bishop Arts District of Dallas, TX. This neighborhood serves him well as it is close to the Oak Lawn neighborhood, where he frequents the Dallas Design Center for work and many of his favorite dens of iniquity for fun. In his home studio, our Otter works his magic as a coveted event planner and wedding designer.

Hotter Otter's abode overflows with a melange of exotic flowers, craft supplies, and display props. He jokingly refers to his studio as "The Unicornicopia." Yet all this gorgeous, day-glo chaos can be concealed in the blink of an eye behind a clever, Otter-designed, movable, loft wall when he needs to meet clients or greet dinner party guests. His design sense is unquestionably refined, but he's not averse to a touch of kitsch. He perches Tiki mugs alongside minimalist Industrial decor without batting an eye.

When he isn't organizing or overseeing a fabulous wedding or fundraiser, Hotter Otter loves hosting memorable dinner parties that feature his fanciful cocktails inspired by mixologists of yesteryear. He jumps at any chance to show off his vintage Georges Briard barware. He takes great pride in his themed gatherings, creating over-the-top tablescapes and evenings of fantasy for his friends and clients.

On weekends, Hotter Otter can be seen leading picnic excursions in the Trinity River Greenbelt or Lake Cliff Park. HO has an affinity for staging elaborate, costumed croquet games and is regarded as a very competitive, and dashing, player.

When Hotter Otter is feeling frisky, he dives into his treasured watering holes—the Dallas Eagle, where he slinks in his leathers, and Hidden Door, where he enjoys the Sunday "Bear" Bust. Always on the cruise for a cute Cub, HO has highly-honed Furdar that stealthily zeroes in on potential mates—the furrier the better.

On Saturdays, Hotter Otter meets his buddies at the Original Market Diner in Northwest Dallas for an old-fashioned, belly-filling breakfast of Ham Steak & Two Eggs in preparation for their serious shopping excursion at the Mothership; Neiman Marcus, in Downtown Dallas. Searching for the latest Fred Perry Polos and J. Lindeberg argyle vests to pair with vintage finds from Zola's stimulates his appetite and makes lunch at Hunky's a must. Hotter Otter likes his catch of Patty Melt and Tater Tots served with one ramekin of mayo and one ramekin of smoky BBQ sauce; he is a self-proclaimed "Condiment Queen." Otters love fish, so you can regularly find this hungry mammal at Screen Door, a Modern Southern kitchen in the Arts District for Chili Fried Catfish and Cast Iron Fried Oysters.

Our energetic Otter must also satisfy his aquatic activity cravings! This calls for pilgrimages to the Rainbow Ranch, a Gay & Lesbian campground in Groesbeck, TX, where he cavorts with his Bear buddies in Lake Limestone. When he seeks water closer to home, Hotter Otter is amazingly resourceful and can always find a hip pool party in the Oak Cliff area.

Hotter Otter's ultimate shindig is TBRU, Texas Bear Round Up, which is quickly becoming the hottest Bear Run in the USA. Every March, HO outfits himself in his sexiest western wear: tight, faded Levi's; vintage, snakeskin, cowboys boots; and an embroidered, snap-button, rodeo shirt. Then he rides to town in his '77 Ford F100 Ranger for a Bear adventure as big as Texas (yes, everything IS big in Texas). You can observe him whooping it up and having the time of his life doing the do-si-do with rugged, or at least rugged-styled, CowBears and Cubs.

Do you wanna two-step with Hotter Otter?

> One of these days I'll plan my own damn wedding and it will be stunning!

1. Assorted fresh flowers from wholesale market
2. Tiki mug collection
3. Virgil's® black cherry cream soda
4. "Retro" Palm® Treo for keeping track of it all
5. Vintage Penguin® button-down shirt
6. Requisite bow tie from Otter's collection
7. Vintage seersucker pants from Zola's
8. Florist sheers

Dominating the wickets, Hotter Otter lines up his infamous "triple peel" at the scenic Trinity Overlook Park.

Food & Drink

Mountain Dew® Throwback (with cane sugar) sets the mood for his White Trash dinner party

Corn Dogs with copious amounts of condiments

Otter Pops®, the perfect palate cleanser

Slim Jim®, the "meat" food group

Potato salad, the "vegetable" food group

Animal cookies, the "delicious" food group

LIKES: Themed dinner parties
DISLIKES: Pickled beets

DALLAS

BARS

1) The Eagle: 5740 Maple Ave • (214) 357-4375 • dallaseagle.com
2) Hidden Door: 5025 Bowser Ave • (214) 526-0620 • hiddendoor-dallas.com
3) The Mining Co: 3903 Cedar Springs Rd • (214) 521-4205 • tmcdallas.com
4) S4 (Station 4): 3911 Cedar Springs Rd • (214) 526-7171 • station4dallas.com

FOOD

5) Chicken Scratch (The Foundry): 2302 Pittman St • (214) 749-1112 • cs-tf.com
6) Dude, Sweet Chocolate: 408 W 8th St • (214) 943-5943 • dudesweetchocolate.com
7) Hunky's: 321 N Bishop Ave • (214) 941-3322 • hunkys.com
8) Mike Anderson's BBQ: 5410 Harry Hines Blvd • (214) 630-0735 • mikeandersonsbbq.com
9) Original Market Diner: 4434 Harry Hines Blvd • (214) 521-0992 • originalmarketdiner.com
10) Smoke: 900 Fort Worth Ave • (214) 393-4141 • smokerestaurant.com
11) Tillman's Roadhouse: 324 W 7th St • (214) 942-0988 • tillmansroadhouse.com

COFFEE

12) Oak Lawn Coffee: 2720 Oak Lawn Ave • (214) 219-5511 • oaklawncoffee.com
13) Oddfellow's: 316 W 7th St • (214) 944-5958 • oddfellowsdallas.com

FURNITURE

14) 20cdesign: 1430 N Riverfront Blvd • (214) 939-1430 • 20cdesign.com
15) Collage 20th Century Classics: 1300 N Riverfront Blvd • (214) 828-9888 • collageclassics.com
16) Jones Walker: 1531 Dragon St • (469) 916-5500 • joneswalkerhome.com

SHOPPING

17) Neiman Marcus: "The Mothership" • 1618 Main St • (214) 741-6911 • neimanmarcus.com
18) The Workroom: 422 Singleton Blvd • (214) 663-0857• theworkroomdallas.com
19) Zola's Vintage: 414 N Bishop Ave • (214) 943-6643 • zolasvintage.com

POINTS OF INTEREST

20) The Belmont Hotel: 901 Fort Worth Ave • (214) 393-2300 • belmontdallas.com
21) Dallas Design Center: Mecca of Interior Design • 1025 N Stemmons Fwy • (214) 242-1600 designcenterdallas.com
22) Lake Cliff Park: Running, hiking, skating trails around a lake surrounded by towering Oak trees 300 E Colorado Blvd • dallasparks.org
23) Rainbow Ranch Campground: Gay and Lesbian campground at Lake Limestone 1662 LCR 800, Groesbeck TX • (254) 729-8484 • rainbowranch.net
24) Trinity River Greenbelt Park: Old ranch roads through dense forest along the river provide a wilderness in the city • 3700 Sylvan • trinityrivercorridor.com

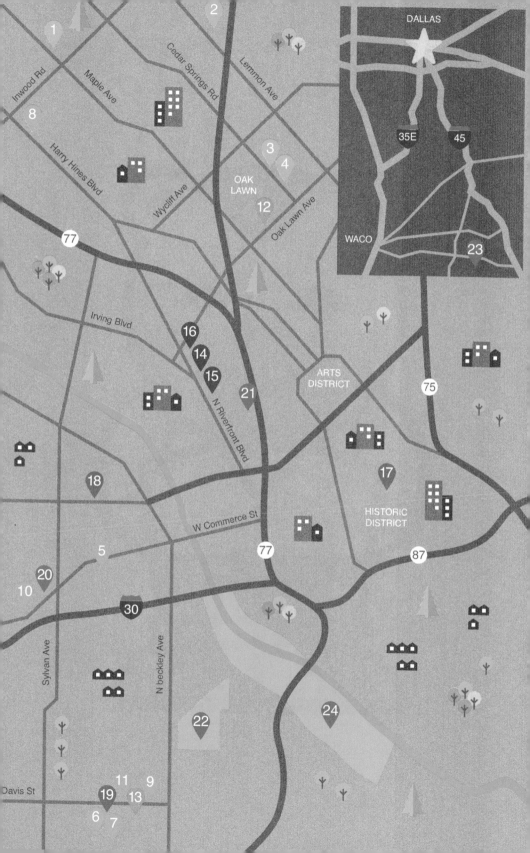

GINGER BEAR

Ginger Bears are prized for their freckle-skinned, fiery-pelted beauty and rugged spirit. *Ursus rufus*, as he's referred to by licensed Bearologists, thrives in temperate climates and heavily shaded or forested environments. Our Ginger Bear typifies the species, residing in Portland, OR and working for the forestry service.

While Portland is chock full of lively neighborhoods that our lumberjack sophisticate loves to frequent, Ginger Bear actually spends most of his days working in Mount Hood National Forest, Portland's wildly impressive backdrop named for Oregon's highest mountain. Happily making his home in a cozy tree house in the woods, Ginger Bear lives a simple, zen-like existence. His 500-square-foot Lair of reclaimed wood functions as a fire lookout tower, and requires him to make everything streamlined and functional.

He has a perfectly edited, Modern furniture collection from local stores, including an orange velvet sofa/bed from Perch Furniture, and a few, favorite, vintage pieces from The Good Mod, like a teak credenza and an orange Eames shell chair. His scant possessions include a little collection of orange knickknacks and utilitarian camping equipment—mostly gifts from friends who find it funny to buy him orange goodies to match his hair, and deluxe gear as a treat for the Bear who gets his water trucked in once a month.

Who knows, maybe one day he'll use a chunk of the "nut" he has squirreled away to buy a spacious pad in the Pearl District. He is frequently spotted in that neighborhood, hanging out with his buds at their favorite coffee spot, Barista, before cheering on Portland's soccer team, the Timbers, at Jeld-Wen Field. Afterward, Ginger Bear and his pack enjoy a rollicking meal at Clyde Common in Portland's Ace Hotel. Roasted Pork, Fresh Corn Grits, Braised Greens and Chili Vinegar hit the spot.

When the night's festivities wind down, GB has no trouble sleeping on a friend's couch, or off-roading in his bio-diesel Jeep Wrangler back to the treehouse to sleep on his.

Ginger Bear's closet is a rustic, wooden, tree branch that hangs from the wall and holds a week's worth of earthy flannel, Pendleton wool, Levi's jeans, and well-worn t-shirts, much of which is from Blake in the Nob Hill area. Just because he's a manly man, choppin' wood and rebuilding hiking trails, doesn't mean he can't appreciate the finer things in life!

Calorie-burning activities work up a Bear-sized appetite, so Ginger Bear heads to the Doug Fir Lounge inside the very retro Jupiter Hotel for a Fir Burger: One-half pound of Beef with Bacon, Gruyere, Garlic Mayo and house made Pickles makes a leisurely feast for this hungry animal. Sometimes GB satisfies his hankerings at Sushi Land. When the Salmon Rolls make their way up the conveyor belt and into his mouth, he feels like a Modern Bear indeed. Ginger Bear is known to order audacious treats at Voodoo Doughnut or homemade ice cream at Salt & Straw when his sweet tooth strikes.

The solitude of the woods often leaves our sweet redhead in the mood for companionship, but Portland Bears face a unique "Furdar" challenge—the lumberjack look is always in fashion here for men of all persuasions! Confident in his Bear senses, he enjoys the friendly scene at Dig a Pony with their soul DJs, or grabs a few delicious draught beers at Eagle Portland on the weekends. And he never misses the monthly Bearracuda party at Boxxes. GB hopes to settle down some day with an outdoorsy "Oso" or Brown Bear as his hiking partner for romantic trips to the Columbia River Gorge and nearby Multnomah Falls. And he can't wait to share all the secrets of his forest.

Do you wanna climb Ginger Bear's tree?

> A trucker will slow down for a Cub and stop for a Wolf, but he'll back up 500 yards for a Ginger Bear!

1. Stanley® thermos of Irish Coffee with Redbreast® whiskey
2. Good ol' compass
3. Trusty Gränsfors Bruks axe
4. Rag & Bone® jeans
5. Work shirt from Blake
6. Asian pottery planters
7. Actual trunk of the tree!
8. Home sweet home / Fire Lookout station
9. Wenger® hiking boots

Creating his own special cardio burn, Ginger Bear chops wood for a romantic, fireside rendezvous in the treehouse.

Food & Drink

Bärenjäger® shot in black tea

Fiesta® dinnerware in non-radioactive orange

Wild-caught Pacific salmon burger

Sweet potato fries & homemade aioli

Unreal 54™ candy

Orange enamel tray from a friend

LIKES: Sweet potato casserole with marshmallow "freckles"
DISLIKES: Artificially dyed orange Salmon

PORTLAND

BARS

1) Boxxes: Bearracuda • 1035 SW Stark St • boxxes.com
2) Dig A Pony: 736 SE Grand Ave • (971) 279-4409 • digaponyportland.com
3) The Eagle: 835 N Lombard St • (503) 283-9734 • eagleportland.com
4) Local Lounge: 3536 NE Martin Luther King Jr Blvd • (503) 282-1833 • local-lounge.com

FOOD

5) Clyde Common: 1014 SW Stark St • (503) 228-3333 • clydecommon.com
6) Doug Fir Lounge: 830 E Burnside St • (503) 231-9663 • dougfirlounge.com
7) Pink Rose: 1300 NW Lovejoy St • (503) 482-2165 • pinkrosepdx.com
8) Pok Pok: 3226 SE Division St • (503) 232-1387 • pokpokpdx.com
9) Salt & Straw: 838 NW 23rd Ave • (971) 271-8168 • saltandstraw.com
10) Sushi Land: 138 NW 10th Ave • (503) 546-9933 • sushilandusa.com
11) Voodoo Doughnut: 22 SW 3rd Ave • (503) 241-4704 • voodoodoughnut.com
12) The Woodsman Tavern: 4537 SE Division St • (971) 373-8264 • woodsmantavern.com

COFFEE

13) Barista: 539 NW 13th Ave • baristapdx.com
14) Coava: 1300 SE Grand Ave • (503) 894-8134 • coavacoffee.com
15) Stumptown Coffee Roasters: 128 SW 3rd Ave • (503) 295-6144 • stumptowncoffee.com

FURNITURE

16) The Good Mod: 1313 W Burnside St • (503) 206-6919 • thegoodmod.com
17) Perch: 923 NW 10th Ave • (503) 208-5128 • perchfurniture.com
18) Portland Modern: 2109 NW Irving St • (503) 243-2580 • pomomodern.com
19) Shag Midcentury (at Sorel): 3713 SE Hawthorne Blvd • 503-232-8482 • shagmidcentury.com

SHOPPING

20) Blake: 26 NW 23rd Pl • (503) 222-4848 • loveblake.tumblr.com

POINTS OF INTEREST

21) Ace Hotel: Portland's unique aesthetic in a boutique hotel • 1022 SW Stark St
(503) 228-2277 • acehotel.com/portland
22) Jupiter Hotel: Mid-century renovated boutique hotel • 800 E Burnside St
(503) 230-9200 • jupiterhotel.com
23) Mt. Hood National Forest: 60 miles of forested mountains, lakes and streams
16400 Champion Way, Sandy • (503) 668-1700
24) Multnomah Falls: Second tallest year-round waterfall in the US
oregon.com/attractions/multnomah_falls

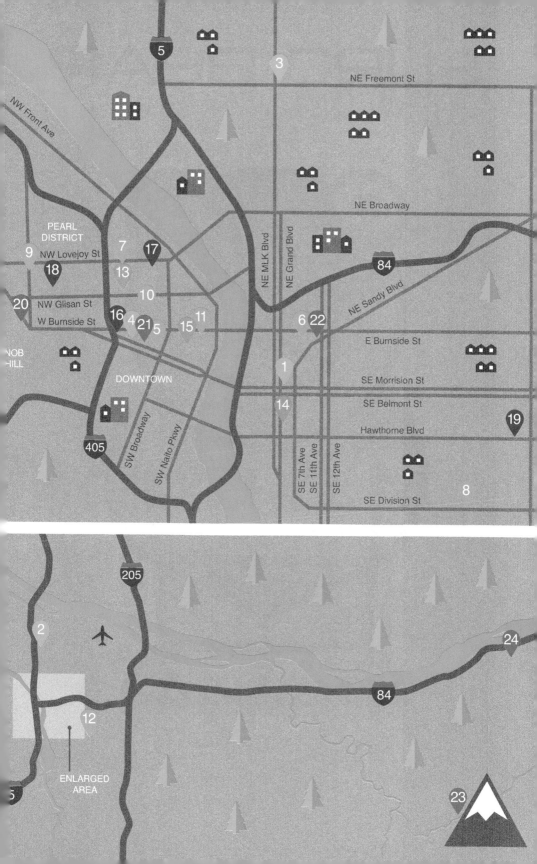

EURO BEAR

We travel to the sun-drenched coast of Spain to explore the habits and habitat of our sultry, swarthy Euro Bear.

It is in the urban wilds of Barcelona that we find this sexy, hairy beast. He inhabits an ultra-chic, all-white, modern Mediterranean villa perched on a high hill just north of the city in Sant Cugat, and funds his life of luxury via a stellar career in international banking and his impressive investment portfolio.

Born and raised on the island of Mallorca, Euro Bear was reared as a privileged Cub. He appreciates the good life and takes pleasure in sharing his good fortune and lavish lifestyle with his friends. His extravagant pool parties are legendary with delectable guests like adult film star Aitor Crash and fashion designer David Delfin. Invitations are highly prized in the Bear community.

Euro Bear unwinds from his busy life as a financier by cavorting and picnicking with his buddies at the full-service, resort-style, gay beach, Platja de la Bossa Rodona in Sitges. This nearby resort town, less than an hour's train ride from Barcelona, features one of the most beautiful stretches along the Mediterranean and is a popular destination for European Bears of all shapes and sizes. English, Scottish, and Irish Bears flock here to escape the cold and rain. Bears of all nationalities come for the sun and fun with likeminded *Ursus gayomous*.

When he's feeling especially adventurous, Euro Bear hops in his Mercedes SLS AMG Coupe and roars down the coast to Playa del Muerto, an exclusively Gay nude beach. Getting there involves a rocky hike, but the trek is well worth the site of Euro Bear basking on his Pucci beach towel, his oiled, dark, furry body glistening in the afternoon sun.

Euro Bear has plenty of lively, favorite haunts for his entertainment pleasures. His first picks are always Bacon Bear Bar and Butch Bear Barcelona, where he meets pals for Sangria de Cava, a locally popular drink made with Spain's delicious sparkling wine.

The ultimate, international Bear party happens right on Euro Bear's home turf. Bearcelona is a hugely popular event held annually in the late Spring. Here you can observe him dancing shirtless until sunrise, encircled by his admiring fans.

Euro Bear's feeding rituals include generous quantities of Paella, Tapas, and Seafood. His treasured hunting grounds include Cal Pep with their elaborate, seasonal Tapas, and La Cova Fumada, where he indulges in their savory Bombas, fried balls of mashed potatoes with tasty meats and spicy pepper sauce.

To offset these foodie feasts, Euro Bear keeps his Muscle-Bear physique in shape at Club Metropolitan in L'Eixample district, affectionately known to locals as "Gayxample." After a burly workout, he cools down in the terrace solarium atop the gymnasium where he takes in the spectacular view of Sagrada Família, Antonio Gaudí's breathtaking basilica.

Fashion is important in Barcelona, even for a Bear. For his banking wardrobe, Euro Bear turns to his friend, Spanish designer "Puri" Garcia, from whom he buys sleek and sophisticated sports jackets and accessories at Purificacion Garcia. His off-hours sexy jeans and tight t-shirts are Diesel Black Gold and Armand Basi. When in Sitges, he loves shopping for provocative swimwear at es4u.

Euro Bear likes treating his dates to a day of fun at Tibidabo, an amusement park perched on the highest hill in Barcelona. They take the Funicular tram to the mountaintop and spend a day of fun on the amusement rides while enjoying the amazing views of the city below.

A romantic at heart, it is not unusual to see Euro Bear enjoying moonlit walks through Las Ramblas, taking in the beauty of Barcelona. If you happen to cross his path, stay calm and utter your best "bona nit." Perhaps you will be favored with one of his pool party invitations.

You do like to skinny dip, don't you?

I've been called a Circuit Bear, but I'm really a homebody who'd rather be cuddling a Papi Bear.

1. Prada® sunglasses (at bottom of hot tub)
2. Cava Rojo, his cocktail of choice
3. Swimsuit from es4u in Sitges
4. Pucci® beach towel

5. David statue from Mercat Del Encants (flea market)
6. Beach ball from El Corte Ingles® (department store)
7. Guide to Gaudi, Barcelona's most famous architect
8. Guest towels

Getting his "bailando" on during Bearcelona, Euro Bear struts his furry stuff at Lust.

Food & Drink

Paella with prawn and mussels

Espresso

Sea salt & lemon pepper

Table by Roger Capron

LIKES: Picnics on the beach
DISLIKES: Sand in the food!

BARCELONA

BARS

1) Lust: Carrer De Casanova 75 • +34 934-514-119
2) Bacon Bear Bar: Carrer De Casanova 64

FOOD

3) Cal Pep: Plaça de les Olles 8 • +34 933-107-961 • calpep.com
4) La Cova Fumada: Calle Baluard 56 • +34 932-214-061
5) Rincon De Pepe: Paseo de la Ribera 35, Sitges • +34 938-945-054 • hotelsitges.com

COFFEE

6) Cafe De L'opera: La Rambla 74 • +34 933-177-585 • cafeoperabcn.com
7) Caffe D'Arts: Carrer Del Bruc 118 • +34 934-587-915
8) Doctor Coffee: Passeig de Sant Joan Bosco 59 • +34 932-059-123 • Doctorcoffee.es

FURNITURE

9) Arkitektura: Via Augusta 185 • +34 933-624-720 • arkitektura.es
10) Bauhaus: Paseo Zona Franca 123 • +34 932-232-112 • bauhaus.es
11) Ici et La: Pasaje Sert 5 • +34 932-687-843 • icietla.com
12) L'appartement: Carrer d'Enric Granados 44 • +34 934-522-904 • lappartement.es

SHOPPING

13) El Corte Ingles: Plaça De Catalunya 14 • +34 933-063-800 • elcorteingles.es
14) eS4U: Sant Pere 5, Sitges • +34 938-110-970
15) Purificacion Garcia: Passeig de Gracia 21 • +34 934-877-292 • purificaciongarcia.com
16) Zara: Passeig de Gracia 16 • +34 933-187-675 • zara.com

POINTS OF INTEREST

17) Club Metropolitan (Gym): Carrer de Provença 408 • +34 935-073-325 • clubmetropolitan.net
18) Park Güell/ Gaudi House Museum: Carrer d'Olot • +34 932-193-811 • casamuseugaudi.org
19) Sagrada Famila: Expansive architectural icon of Barcelona and Gaudi's most impassioned work • Carrer de Mallorca 401 • +34 932-073-031 • sagradafamilia.cat
20) Sagrat Cor at Tibidabo: Neogothic cathedral atop Barcelona's tallest peak • carretera de Vallvidrera al Tibidabo 71 • +34 932-117-942 • tibidabo.cat
Sitges Beaches:
21) Playa Balmins: nudist beach, straight and gay
22) Platja de la Bassa Rodona: popular clothed gay beach
23) Playa Del Muerto: cove-secluded gay nude beach
24) Tibidabo: Mountaintop amusement park with views of Barcelona and the Mediterranean. Reached by funicular train • tibidabo.cat

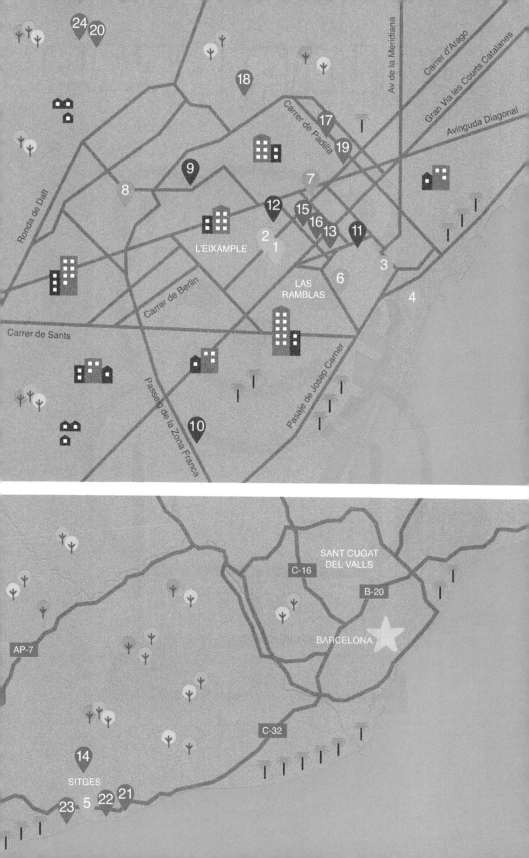

POLAR BEAR

Polar Bears in the Arctic may be an endangered species, but the contrary is true in Chicago where the winters go sub-zero and the summers are over the top. Our specimen thrives in this cosmopolitan environment on Lake Michigan with its vibrant population of silver and white-haired bears amongst Chicago's enormous Gay community.

Our handsome, hardworking Polar Bear has crafted a cultured gourmand's ideal life as the owner and executive chef of his own culinary empire in Chicago's tony Riverview North neighborhood. His restaurants, cafés, and gastropubs are popular Windy City destinations known for delicious, comforting offerings and stylish, Modern interiors.

From Jerry Mathers to Ann Sather, Polar Bear has been influenced by the hardworking, middle-class values that shaped the great culture of Chicagoland and the Midwest. As a child, his father took him to the now kitschy, yet iconic, Ann Sather Restaurant for a breakfast of Swedish Pancakes. A chance meeting with the stoic, Swedish lady sparked PB's desire to learn all he could about food and forged his restaurateur identity. With a scholarship to the Culinary Academy, he was on his way to becoming one of Chicago's beloved chefs, and Chicagoans LOVE food.

Typical of restaurant folk, Polar Bear is married to his work, but now that he largely manages his business operations, he makes time to indulge his other loves—art and architecture. He is frequently seen admiring the architecturally significant buildings of downtown Chicago, or taking in the latest exhibit at the Art Institute, often with Muscle Bear on his arm. Several weekends a year, Muscle Bear flies from LA to play with Polar Bear and the two make a stunning Bearnamic Duo.

From a lifetime spent in his chef whites, Polar Bear is not much of a clothes horse, but he enjoys watching Muscle Bear try on form-enhancing, tailored LBM 1911 suits at Haberdash.

Afterward, they go for beard stylings at the nearby Esquire Barbershop. When solo, Polar Bear prowls for perfect accoutrements for his Bear Lair, a loft condo on Lakeshore Drive's Gold Coast that he keeps neat as a pin. He regularly visits his favorite hunting grounds, Post 27, Scout, and his local Design Within Reach. He is particularly fond of I.D. Chicago, where the amazing staff helped him with both his home décor and several of his restaurant interiors.

Taking a break from ordering fresh ingredients and eclectic wines, Polar bear heads to neighboring Hub 51 for an inspired meal of Brussels Sprout Salad and a Turkey Meatloaf Sandwich. The owners fondly greet our Bear and talk shop; he's testing ideas for a sleek, new take on comfort food that he has gleefully named "2045." What will pot roast and macaroni and cheese look and taste like in the future anyway?

On occasion, Polar Bear ventures into the local wilds for an evening of fun. He enjoys Big Chicks' friendly atmosphere and savory BBQ at Bear Den on Thursday nights. On the wilder weekends, he treks to The Cell Block's Furr Party for some eye candy and pelt rubbing. This restaurateur also knows how to throw a party, and each spring he hosts spectacular events at his restaurants to coincide with Chicago's Bear Pride Weekend.

Polar bear looks damn good in a sweater so naturally he has taken up skiing! He and Muscle Bear rendezvous for Bears on Skis at Elevation Mammoth, the third largest Gay Ski weekend of the year. PB flies to LA and grabs his gorgeous cohort for an adventurous ride along the eastern side of the Sierra Nevadas. They always book a scenic room in the "chalet-tastic" Mammoth Mountain Inn which retains much of its Mid-century, retro charm. The après-ski events give Polar Bear a chance to show off his silvery, sexy physique on the dance floor, in the hot tub, and on the town!

Who you calling Daddy? Polar Bear, that's who.

> Food can be just as good as sex—in fact, I've got a mirror over my kitchen table!

1. 2007 Flor De Pingus Ribera del Duero
2. Vinotemp® bottle opener
3. Apron from Restaurant Depot®
4. Saveur® and Food Network® magazines
5. Blue Eames® Eiffel-base chair from An Orange Moon
6. Herman Miller® LED Leaf-light from I.D. Chicago
7. Black leather Wassily chair from Interior Express Outlet
8. PB's old school Rolodex® that he's had since culinary school
9. Black pants from Haberdash

Toning his muscles, as well as his taste buds, Polar Bear pumps himself up to explore all the sensual adventures Chicago has to offer.

Food & Drink

Saarinen® tulip table with Eames® chairs

Chicken Pot Pie with marjoram & celery (his new recipe)

Voss® sparkling water (glass bottle only!)

Fancy mixed nuts in Tapia Wirkkala bowl

Puilly-fuissé wine

Grappa Julia (for desert!)

Black lacquer tray from West Elm®

LIKES: Hormone-free chicken
DISLIKES: Hormone-injected men

CHICAGO

BARS

1) Big Chicks: 5024 N Sheridan Rd • (773) 728-5576 • bigchicks.com
2) Cellblock: Furr Party • 3702 N Halsted St • (773) 665-8064 • cellblock-chicago.com
3) Jackhammer: 6406 N Clark St • (773) 743-5772 • jackhammer-chicago.com
4) Touché: 6412 N Clark St • (773) 465-7400 • touchechicago.com

FOOD

5) Ann Sather: 909 W Belmont • (773) 348-2378 • annsather.com
6) Big Jones: 5347 N Clark St • (773) 275-5725 • bigjoneschicago.com
7) Harry Caray's Steakhouse: 33 W Kinzie St • (312) 828-0962 • harrycarays.com
8) Hub 51: 51 W Hubbard St • (312) 828-0021 • hub51chicago.com
9) Nookies Tree: 3334 N Halsted St • (773) 248-9888 • nookiesrestaurants.net
10) Owen & Engine: 2700 N Western Ave • (773) 235-2930 • owenandengine.com

COFFEE

11) Big Shoulders Coffee: 1105 W Chicago Ave • (312) 888-3042 • bigshoulderscoffee.com
12) Caffe Streets: 1750 W Division St • (773) 278-2739 • caffestreets.com
13) First Slice Pie: 5357 N Ashland Ave • (773) 275-4297 • firstslice.org

FURNITURE

14) An Orange Moon: 2418 W North Ave • (312) 450-9821 • anorangemoon.com
15) I.D. Chicago: 3337 N Halsted St #1 • (773) 755-4343 • idchicago.com
16) Post 27: 1819 W Grand Ave • (312) 829-6122 • post27store.com
17) Scout: 5221 North Clark St • (773) 275-5700 • scoutchicago.com

SHOPPING

18) Bears Like Us: 3732 N Broadway • (773) 857-7393 • bearslikeus.com
19) Esquire Barber Shop: Beard trim • 1511 W Foster Ave • (773) 754-0953
20) Haberdash: 607 N. State St • (312) 624-8551 • haberdashmen.com
21) Leather 6410/Paul C Leathers: 6410 N Clark St • (800) 910-0666 • paulcleather.com

POINTS OF INTEREST

23) Art Institute of Chicago: Architecture and design galleries feature works by Frank Lloyd Wright, Ludwig Mies van der Rohe, and Bruce Goff • artic.edu
22) Boystown: First officially recognized Gay Village in the US. Located within Lakeview neighborhood. Cultural center for one of the largest LGBT communities in the nation. Lively, late-night bar scene.
24) Leather Archives Museum: Comprehensive and fascinating library, museum and archives of leather culture • leatherarchives.org
25) Robie House: Frank Lloyd Wright house on University of Chicago campus, considered one of the most important buildings in american architecture and a forerunner of modernism • gowright.org
26) Mammoth Mountain Inn: Elevation Mammoth Gay Ski Week • 1001 Minaret Rd, Mammoth Lakes, CA • (760) 934-2581 • themammothmountaininn.com

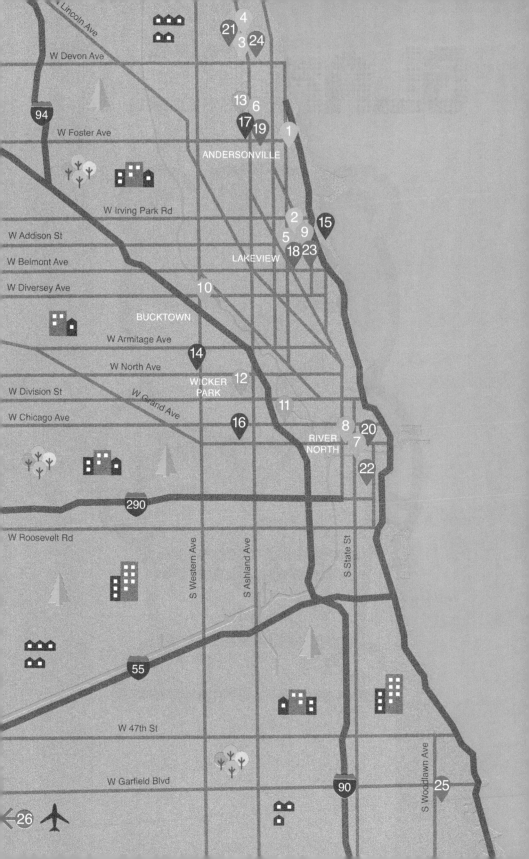

GLAM BEAR

A rare crossbreed, *Ursus glamoramous*, or Glam Bear, can only be found in Gay captivity. Our London-based specimen is a unique combination of Bear and Circuit Gay - he's Bond... Bear Bond. Jet-setting around the globe is second nature to Glam Bear with his fabulous career in the airline industry. He's created a sophisticated, untethered lifestyle most of us have only dreamt of. "A bear in every port," is his motto.

Glam Bear has established his habitat in Vauxhall, which he cheekily refers to as the "Bearmuda Triangle." There, you can observe him in his sleek, modern Bearchelor pad, complete with wet-bar and a swingin' '60s, circular bed... that rotates!

When he's not traveling, our Playbear takes advantage of all the nightlife London has to offer. You may spot him catching up with his buddies at Comptons of Soho, where GB loves spending a Saturday afternoon with his Pimm's Cups and his Bear posse, watching the other creatures of the city go by.

Afterwards, he staggers across the street to the conveniently located Balans, one of his favorite restaurants, where he devours Toulouse Sausages and Garlic-rosemary Mash. Tasty food and tasty waiters—what more could a Bear ask for?

If he's not airborne on a Saturday night, Glam Bear enjoys the Royal Vauxhall Tavern, South London's oldest existing Gay venue, for their authentic, London honky-tonk party, Duckie. There, he sips a martini or two, taking in a drag show and regaling his friends with his latest amorous adventures. After-hours, GB saunters to Hoist, a kinky, cruise bar with an interesting (and enforced) dress code; "Boots or trainers with jocks, shorts, or pants. Naked if you dare."

Glam Bear has a great love for art and theater. He adores catching a show in London's Theaterland, the largest theater district in the world.

You may spy him in a balcony seat, splendidly attired in his Prada tuxedo, opera glasses in hand, with a handsome young Cub on his arm.

Glam Bear's three main passions are sex, shopping, and going to the gym. On more than one occasion, he has accomplished all three simultaneously! He's a self-described "Gym Bunny," spending hours at Paris Gym with his trainer. He also loves to play rugby, a sport he learned in his prep school days. More than the sport itself, Glam Bear likes how he fills out his rugby shorts and the effect this has on his onlookers.

After his weekday workouts, GB meets his buds for coffee at Covent Garden and shopping at Harvey Nichols, a store that originally opened in the 1880s and is now considered a Gay institution. On a good day, cruising eight floors devoted to fashion, home décor, and dining can rival sex for Glam Bear's favorite activity.

On the weekends, Glam Bear loves lazy, luxurious brunches at the Delaunay or torrid gossip sessions over coffee at the top of the Tate Modern. In the afternoon he heads to Camden Market where he uses his stealth shopping skills to pick up a vintage rugby ball for his Bearchelor pad at Original Vintage Luggage. Yes it can be touristy, but he is in and out like a flash and smoothly scores a veggie samosa from a street vendor as a treat for his impressive efficiency.

When globetrotting, Glam Bear delights in visiting his favorite international hot spots. He adores the sophisticated Café Retro in Lugano Switzerland with their cozy piano bar, elegant ambiance, and signature Rossini Steak. If there is a beach to be found, you'll catch Glam Bear on it. He especially digs the sands at Ipanema in Rio de Janeiro. Standing out from all the eye candy on the gay stretch of beach, Glam Bear is resplendent in his Tom Ford swimsuit and sunglasses.

Would you mind rubbing a little suntan oil onto the bits Glam Bear can't reach?

In my line of work, I'm much more into the "lay" than the "over."

1. Handcuffs from his personal collection
2. Jock strap left by last night's date
3. Room service
4. Tea time! Fortnum & Mason® Earl Grey Classic loose leaf tea
5. Black trousers from Next in Covent Garden
6. Ben Sherman® tie
7. Pimm's No.1® liqueur
8. Pimm's Cup with Palmers Ginger Beer and lemon cucumber garnish
9. Apple iPhone®—Glam Bear's worldwide "little black book!"

Returning home to London, Glam Bear heads to Hyde Park for a ruck in the muck with his rugby mates.

Food & Drink

Cedar planked Icelandic salmon with maple glaze

Organic field greens

Rosé (all out of Riesling on the flight)

Pistachios and Paul A. Young dark chocolate truffle

LIKES: Caipirinhas in Sao Paolo
DISLIKES: Missed workouts anywhere

LONDON

BARS

1) The Eagle: 349 Kennington Lane • +44 20-7793-0903 • eaglelondon.com
2) The Hoist: Arches 47C South Lambeth Rd • +44 20-7735-9972 • thehoist.co.uk
3) The Kings Arms: 23 Poland St • +44 20-7734-5907
4) Profile: 84-86 Wardour St • +44 20-7734-3444 • profilesoho.com
5) Royal Vauxhaul Tavern: 372 Kennington Lane • +44 20-7820-1222 • rvt.org.uk

FOOD

6) Balans: 60-62 Old Compton St • +44 20-7439-2183 • balans.co.uk
7) Comptons: 51-53 Old Compton St • +44 20-3238-0163 • faucetinn.com
8) The Delaunay: 55 Aldwych • +44 20-7499-8558 • thedelaunay.com
9) Elliot's: Borough Market • 12 Stoney St • +44 29-7403-7436 • elliotscafe.com
10) J. Sheekey Oyster Bar: 28-32 St Martin's Ct • +44 20-7240-2565 • j-sheekey.co.uk
11) Patisserie Valerie: 44 Old Compton St • 44-20-7437-3466 • patisserie-valerie.co.uk
12) St. John Bar & Restaurant: 26 St John Street • +44 20-3301-8069 • stjohnrestaurant.com

FURNITURE

13) The Conran Shop: Michelin House, 81 Fulham Rd • +44 20-7589-7401 • conranshop.co.uk
    Mid-Century Online (delivery only): online • +44 20-3129-7965 • mid-centuryonline.com
14) Original Vintage Luggage: Unit D37 Camden Stables Market• 078-5093-6469 (mobile)
    londonvintageluggage.com
15) Paere Dansk: 13 Stratford Rd • +44 77-7186-1939 • paeredansk.com

SHOPPING

16) Harvey Nichols: 109-125 Knightsbridge • +44 20-7235-5000 • harveynichols.com/london
17) Primark: 499 Oxford St • +44 20-7495-0420 • primark.co.uk
18) Orla Keily: 31 Monmouth St, Covent Garden • +44 20-7240-4022 • orlakiely.com
19) Selfridges: 400 Oxford St • +44 113-369-8040 • selfridges.com

POINTS OF INTEREST

20) Camden Town: Eclectic market area comprised of Camden Lock Market (crafts galore),
    Camden Stables Market (alternative fashion), Buck Street Market and Inverness Street
    Market • camdenlock.net
21) Covent Garden: First-century settlement turned 17th century fruit market, now a bustling
    area of shops, cafés, pubs and the Royal Opera House • coventgardenlondonuk.com
22) The Geffrye Museum: English middle-class living rooms from 1600 to the present, depicted
    through furnishings, textiles, paintings and decorative arts. 136 Kingsland Road
    +44 20-7739-9893 • Geffrye-museum.org.uk
23) Hyde Park/Kensington Gardens: Royal parks in central London that lead to Kensington
    Palace • royalparks.org.uk
24) Portobello Road: World's largest antiques market • portobelloroad.co.uk
25) Tate Modern: Bankside • +44 20-7887-8888 • tate.org.uk

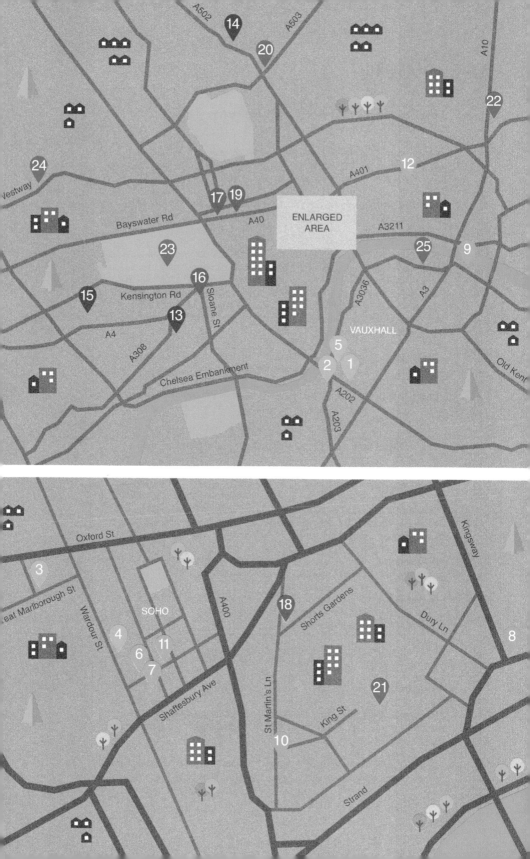

Glossary

A-List Bear: High-profile or exceedingly popular Bear, e.g. Bear DJ, Bear film star/model.

Alterna-Gay: Gay person who leads an alternative lifestyle to the limited, mainstream stereotype of Gay. The Silver Lake neighborhood of L.A. is populated with Alterna-Gays. Also, the gay version of a Hipster.

Bear Chaser: A male who does not fall into any Bear category, but who exhibits a marked physical attraction for Bears. Be careful boys, not all Bears like being chased.

Bear Code: Formerly known as the Natural Bear Classification System, a set of abbreviated terms created by/for Bears in order to communicate their sexual proclivities while protecting their innocence and identity in "adult" classifieds and the new, vast and scary worldwide web of the not-so-distant 1990s. For example; B4 s- D+ +k = Reasonably thick beard, cub tendencies, definite Daddy (endowment gets emphasis), kinky factor. And that was an EASY one! Aren't we glad to be proud and accepted.

Bear Flag: Designed by Craig Barnes in 1995 to symbolize inclusion and the Brotherhood of Bears through colors representing the human race.

Bear Food: Belly-filling, comfort-inducing nourishment commonly consumed in the form of cheeseburgers, sloppy joe's, macaroni and cheese, and other tasty treats stashed in a Bear's larder.

Bear in Beard Only: Nice beard, seal bod. Any questions? See Seal.

Bear Lair: Just as a bear in nature has his cave, a Bear in the human world has his lair, decorated in must-have Bear accessories. A Bear's Lair is his Castle.

Bear Run: Also called Bear Gathering. Events such as Bear Week, Lazy Bear Weekend, Texas Bear Round-Up and others. Popular destination spots for many varietals of Bears and their fans.

Bear Week: The MotherBear of all Bear Runs. A week devoted to Bears Gone Wild in the charming, oceanside city of Provincetown (P-Town), MA.

Bearbucks: Nickname for Starbucks coffee houses largely patronized by Bears and located in serious Bear neighborhoods, e.g. Ansley Mall Bearbucks in Atlanta, The Castro Bearbucks in San Francisco.

Bearcelona: Hugely popular, international Bear Run in Barcelona, Spain. Annual, six-day extravaganza for fur lovers.

Bear-aoke: Popular karaoke events patronized by Bears.

Bearmuda Triangle: Concentrated area of Bear activity configured between three strategic points, e.g. Silver Lake's gayborhood parameters are drawn between the Eagle LA, Faultline, and Akbar.

Bearnamic Duo: WonderBear Powers... Activate! Bearnamic Duos have "that" relationship. Loving, fur-covered couple, generally sticky sweet and highly envied.

Bearracuda: One of the most largely attended, nationwide, Bear dance parties in the U.S. Their motto is "A fun, friendly party for bears, cubs, and other wildlife."

Bearrage: A sudden gathering of bears in one location; a flash mob, but with a lot more fur.

Bearrah Pawcett: '70s Farrah has nothing on her Bearrah-licious counterpart! First spotted at the 2011 Provincetown Bear Week where her stunning blonde locks and amazingly furry bod were a bombshell hit.

Bears in Space: Popular, monthly, Bear disco held at Akbar in Los Angeles, CA.

Bears in the Park: Frequent, casual, and delicious Bear gatherings in Dolores Park, a popular, public destination in the Mission Dolores neighborhood of San Francisco.

Biker Bear: Bear who rides a big, hot motorcycle, i.e. WOOF!

Blow Off: Created and co-DJ'd by partners Bob Mould and Rich Morel. Nationally touring Bear party that attracts a diverse following of music-lovers. Hipsters, beer-drinking men's men, leather daddies and the signature Muscle Bears from Blow Off's graphic artwork unite on the dance floor to bump, grind, dance and enjoy.

Brown Bear: Typically, a Latino, Chicano or Hispanic Bear or *Oso*.

Canis Lupus: Latin for Gray Wolf.

Chelsea Boy: East Coast equivalent of a WeHo Boy, inhabiting the Chelsea neighborhood of Manhattan. Often found cruising near the High Line in search of a Daddy Bear. Like his West Hollywood kin, the Chelsea Boy rarely leaves his habitat, limiting career and social opportunities, but some find Bear or Daddy chasing a full-time job.

Chicago Bear Pride Weekend: Chicago Bear run held Memorial Day Weekend. Annually coincides with International Mr. Leather. Convenient!

Cigar Daddy: Male exhibiting Daddy characteristics who partakes in smoking cigars, i.e. WOOF!

Cub: A young Bear, most likely in his early bearhood. A small Bear. Less frequently, refers to sexual proclivity for being a Bear Bottom.

Daddy Bear: A Bear "of a certain age" or featuring the most classic, masculine Bear attributes but not necessarily belonging to that age group. Sometimes interchangeable with HusBear, ex. "Daddy Bear will be home from work soon, so I had better put on my jock strap and have dinner ready."

Elevation Mammoth: Gay ski week in Mammoth Lakes, CA. Beautiful spring skiing with gregarious, unpretentious Gays and their friends. Laid back, friendly social events in addition to great dance parties.

Furdar: Internal radar detection system that aids Bear seekers in the hunt for furry playmates.

Gayborhood: Neighborhood featuring a large Gay population, e.g. West Hollywood, Midtown Atlanta.

Ginger Bear: Bear with red or auburn-hued pelt and/or facial hair, i.e. WOOF!

Glamping: Glamorous version of camping, i.e. lodging in a luxuriously appointed "tent" with gourmet meals and spa services. Definitely not roughing it!

Grizzly Adams: A man with a furry body and/or face who does not self-identify as a Bear, but is an admirer of Bears. A popular '70s TV show starring Dan Haggerty.

Grizzly Bear: An extremely hirsute Bear, much furrier than average. Has fur all over his body, including back, shoulders, and knuckles.

GROWLr: Popular Bear "meet-up" app for smartphones. Bear analog of Grindr.

Gym Bunny: One who dedicates much of his or her life to working out at the Gym. God bless ya!

HiBearNation: St. Louis Bear run in the Show-Me state with fun annual themes. Four days of parties and events with furry Bears from around the world. Southern HiBearNation is held annually in Melbourne, Australia.

High Heel Drag Race: Annual DC street race in Dupont Circle. Thousands of spectators line 17th Street, the Tuesday before Halloween, to watch fabulously-costumed contestants haul ass in heels.

Honey Bear: Bear equivalent of a sugar daddy. A wealthy Bear who lavishes gifts and trips on a less financially advantaged plaything. Ex. "My Honey Bear bought me these leather boots the first time he flew me to Berlin."

Hot Lynx: Lynx + gym bunny bod = Hot Lynx. See Lynx.

HusBear: Furry man of your dreams, the one you can't live without. Bear version of Husband.

IML: Leather-clad contests, conventions and cruising that culminates in naming International Mr. Leather of the year. Leather, leather and more leather—hot. See Chicago Bear Pride Weekend.

Lazy Bear Weekend: One of the original Bear Runs, held each August on the Russian River in Guerneville, CA; North of San Francisco. Religiously attended by Bay Area Bears.

Lynx: Female version of Modern Bear. Woman with a sporty look and often fuller figure. Not quite butch, not quite femme, but with the goodhearted personality and accepting nature of a bear. Unlike Goldy Lox, Lynx likes the ladies, and they like her - meow!

Mad.Bear: International meeting of "Bears, Big Men and Admirers" held annually in Madrid, Spain.

ManPanion: Male companion in a romantically intimate relationship. Sometimes a precursor term to HusBear.

Momma Bear or Den Mother: Term of affection for a "Mom" type figure in a Bear "family." Female parent of a Bear.

MovieBears: Popular social activity groups around the country for Bears and their friends dedicated to viewing theatrical movie releases, e.g. Phoenix MovieBears, Minneapolis MovieBears.

Muscle Cub: "Cub," from Old English *cubbe* meaning young bear. "Muscle," from Latin *musculus* meaning OMG he has a super hot bod!

Otter Splash AKA Summer Tramp: Annual L.A. Pride event featuring water attractions, entertainment, Otters, and their friends.

Papi Bear: See Daddy Bear, but know that *este es todo Latino*.

Piggy: Bear known to be especially fond of romps in the sack. Yes, this little piggy likes sex in the Bear lair—now, more, and always. Not that there's anything wrong with that. Oink! Oink!

Playbear: Perennially single, bachelor Bear who enjoys playing the field, and stream. Bear version of a Playboy.

Pocket Bear: Diminutively-sized Bear, so adorable and petite you want to put him in your pocket and take him home.

Pup: Young wolf, most likely in his early wolfhood. Term of endearment for a younger male, as in, "Bring daddy a beer, Pup!"

Seal: Semi-popular singer from the 1990s. Also, a sleek and smooth man, having no body fur.

Sloth: Var. Sleuth, the actual term for a group of Bears in the wild. From Middle English *Slowth*. A group of Polar Bears is called a Celebration. Now that's more like it!

Lone Star: Opened in 1989, possibly the first and probably the most archetypal Bear Bar, located in SoMa, San Francisco.

Tiki Bear: Bear Tikiphile—fan of all things Tiki, i.e. Polynesian restaurants, Tiki bars, Shag artwork, Tiki mugs, '60s ukelele albums, and vintage Hawaiian shirts.

Trapper: Male, usually small in stature, who is attracted to Bears or Otters.

Twink: Gay subset that is opposite of a Bear in appearance and mannerisms. May or may not be underage, and/or under the influence of currently popular pharmaceuticals.

Ursus Gayomous: "Latin" term we made up just for this book. *Ursus*, from actual Latin, means Bear. *Gayomous* means, well, Gay!

Valley of the Bears: Sparkle, Bears, Sparkle! You've got to climb Mount Everest to reach the Valley of the Bears. That's just what our Modern Bear models did in 2011, posing for a campy-risqué photo shoot as Neely O'Beara, Mann Welles, and Brentifur North.

WeHo Boy: Is Gold's Gym your second home? Do you stay west of La Brea at all cost? Love The Abbey? Congratulations, you're a WeHo Boy! West Hollywood has more male go-go dancers per capita than any other city on earth. You're probably a pup, twink, muscle cub, or possibly a glam bear and that's OK. Be proud! You work in "the industry," carrying a clipboard, but it sounds good to your friends back home so who cares. Don your short shorts, boys; let's dance till dawn! WeHo boys travel in flocks and love having a few Goldy Loxes in their ranks.

WOOF: Sexy, guttural utterance from one Bear to another signifying admiration and attraction for the other's physical appearance.

About the Authors

Travis Smith is Modern Bear and co-founder of Modern Bear Media, a multi-media company devoted to Modern Design, Bears and Beefcake. He describes himself as a Mid Century Modernist addicted to vintage cars, barbecue cuisine and pop culture. Travis also authored the retro-cult favorite, *Kitschmasland*, a must-have coffee table book for anyone who longs for or lived through Christmas culture of the '50s, '60s & '70s.

I'm searching for spiritual enlightenment and the next fabulous find at an estate sale. I also make a mean Sloppy Joe Bake and Peach Cobbler. ~ Travis Smith

Chris Bale is Design Wolf and co-founder of Modern Bear Media. Interior design and Mid Century Real Estate fuel and inspire him. He views life from a unique perspective and creates expressive images through the lens of his camera and memorable environments through interior design. He also loves to conjure ideas and creative solutions for the aesthetically-motivated Bear.

I'd like to live in a utopia of monorails and mid-century decorated houses, but I'll settle for a tasty meal and some masterful mixology in a well-designed space. ~ Chris Bale

Both Travis and Chris admire fine form, whether in architecture, art, design, or a well-developed member of the Bear family that exemplifies all of the above.

They work continuously to keep Modern Bear exciting and informative. They are currently expanding Modern Bear's online community by developing a travel and lifestyle website, based on *Guide for the Modern Bear*, and an online Modern Bear store.

Stay in the know at:
www.modernbear.net
www.facebook.com/modernbear
www.twitter.com/modernbear

Contributor Directory

Book Design and Illustration -
Jason Hill
Jason Hill Design
hello@jasonhilldesign.com
www.jasonhilldesign.com

Copy Editor, Proofreader and
Fact Checker - Michelina Matarrese
Brainy Lady Book Finishing
michelina.m@me.com

Photography - Leland Gebhardt
Leland Gebhardt Photography
info@lelandg.com
www.lelandg.com

Ginger Bear photography -
Rey Rey's Photography
reyreysphotography.com

Glossary, Directory - Jan Stevens
Redmond Business Solutions
Graphic Design - Creative Advertising,
Marketing - Social Media Strategy
jan@redmondbusinesssolutions.com
www.redmondbusinesssolutions.com

First Edition Editor - Susan Hacker
Redmond Business Solutions, LLC
Project Management
susan@myredmondonline.com
www.redmondbusinesssolutions.com

Legal Services -
Angela Valente Romeo, Esq
Palm Springs CA 92262

Models

Andy Jamison - Muscle Bear
Brendan McWeeney - Ginger Bear
Brent Cage - Glam Bear
Chris Bale - Design Wolf
Heather Budde - Goldy Lox
Henry Lien - Panda Bear
Jeff Cooper - Club Cub
Marvin Jones - Black Bear
Richard Rivera - Tiki Bear
Rich Kraft - Leather Bear
Steve Ruby - Polar Bear
Steven Rezentes - Euro Bear
Tally Duke Floyd - Hotter Otter
Travis Smith - Modern Bear

Furniture, Set Design, Locations

Chamberlain West Hollywood Hotel
1000 Westmount Dr
West Hollywood CA 90069
(310) 657-7400

Modern Manor
Ryan Durkin
716 West Hazelwood St
Phoenix AZ 85013
(602) 266-3376
www.modernmanorstore.com

Phoenix Metro Retro
Douglas and Heidi Abrahamson
708 W Hazelwood St
Phoenix AZ 85013
(602) 279-0702
www.phoenixmetroretro.com

Reclaimed Light Studio
Allen Enochs-White
Phoenix AZ
(602) 626-7900

River View Garden Resort
Monte Rio CA
www.riverviewgardenresort.com

Wil Stiles
Wil Stiles and Molly Bondhus
875 N Palm Canyon Dr
Palm Springs CA 92262
(760) 327-9764
www.wilstiles.com

William Stewart Designs, Inc.
349 Peachtree Hills Ave NE, Ste B-3
Atlanta GA 30305
(404) 816-2501

Accidental Bear
Queer News, Art, Culture
& Discussion
www.accidentalbear.com

Ace Hotel, Palm Springs
www.acehotel.com/palmsprings

Bear Bones Clothing
"For when chest hair just won't
cover it!"
www.bearbonesclothing.com

Bear Gear USA
Bear Clothing, Art, & Bling
www.beargearusa.com

Bearracuda
Bear dance party in 25 cities and counting
bearracuda.com

Bear World Magazine
Monthly online magazine devoted to
everything Bear
www.bearworldmagazine.com

BigMuscleBears
www.bigmusclebears.com

Blake Little Photography
www.blakelittle.com

Blow Off
Famed Bob Mould & Richard Morel
DJ party
blowoff.us

Celebration Theatre
Oldest, continuously-running, professional
theatre in the US serving the GLBT
community
celebrationtheater.com

Christopher Latham
Massage, Music, Energy, Guitar
Topheruby@gmail.com
www.buck25.com

Crandall Mobile RV Service, Inc.
Desert Hot Springs CA 92240
(760) 604-1598
www.crandallmobilervservice.com

Cub Meat
A monthly party for BEARS, CUBS, & OTTERS
in Palm Springs, CA cubMeat.com

D.C. Bear Crüe Happy Hour
"The Nation's Largest Weekly Bear Event"
Hosted by Charger Stone
www.dcbearcrue.com

Glass Garage Art Gallery (Panda Bear)
414 N Robertson Blvd
West Hollywood CA 90048
(310) 659-5228
info@glassgaragegallery.com
www.glassgaragegallery.com

The Greg Gill Company
"Saving Friends from Car Dealers since 1992."
thegreggillcompany.com

Heather Budde (Goldy Lox)
Parnian Interiors
heather@parnian.com
www.parnian.com

Intuitive Touch Massage by Jon
Jon Borges
(480) 862-0000
ntuitivebodywork@aol.com
www.intuitivetouchbyjon.massagetherapy.com

Just Fabulous Bookstore
515 N Palm Canyon Dr
Palm Springs CA 92262
(760) 864-1300

Just Modern
New, Mid-century-modern-inspired home
accessories, art, furniture and decor
justmoderndecor.com

Keller Williams Lifestyle Realty
Matthew Hoedt & Bill Mitchell
Chris Bale's (Design Wolf) Green Team
3540 E Baseline Rd #120
Phoenix AZ 85042
(602) 573-0700
www.chrisbalesgreenteam.com

Lazy Bear Weekend
Bear run held in Guerneville CA since 1995,
and not-for-profit organization committed
to supporting the LGBT community
www.lazybearweekend.com

Modern Bear Directory

Mary Powers (Psychic to the Bears)
Powers of the Light
www.powersofthelight.com

Mountain Bear Crafts
Custom Embroidered Gifts & Products
Van Morrow
www.mountainbearcrafts.com

Palm Springs Massage Therapy
Personal Healing & Restoration
Gregory Bessmer
www.palmspringsmassagetherapy.com

Paul Kaplan Modern Real Estate Group
Mid-century, architectural and vacation
properties in Palm Springs
www.paulkaplanrealtor.com

Past Perfect
San Francisco CA
www.pastperfectsf.com

Rey Rey's Photography
Portrait, Head Shot, Baby
& Pet Photography
www.reyreysphotography.com

Richard Kraft (Leather Bear)
Model for digital portraiture, commercial
print and film
richardbkraft@gmail.com

River View Garden Resort
Monte Rio CA
www.riverviewgardenresort.com

Roman Udulov
www.thegentleofmen.com

Rustyspot Design
Scott McGillivray - Graphic Design
Email: rustyspotdesign@gmail.com

Schuster Printing
1022 E Vista Del Cerro Dr
Tempe AZ 85281
(480) 951-8878
Pablo Ramirez III
www.schustercompany.com

Smarty Paints
Bold, graphic murals and
fashion-forward decorative arts
San Francisco CA
www.smartypaints.biz
smartypaints@me.com

Sonoma Nesting Co.
Guerneville CA
www.sonomanesting.com

Steven Rezentes (Euro Bear)
Available for modeling and photo sessions
rezentessj@gmail.com

Texas Bear Round-Up
Annual Bear Run in Dallas TX -
"Party with a Purpose" for 3 charities
www.tbru.org

Where The Bears Are
Popular, comedy/mystery web series about
the exploits of three Bear roommates
wherethebearsare.tv

William Cabrera
Gay Men's Chorus of Los Angeles
9056 Santa Monica Blvd #300
West Hollywood CA 90069
(424) 239-6514
mailroom@gmcla.org
www.gmcla.org

Nonprofit Organizations

The Emerald Kingdom
Fundraising for Gay Youth Charities
Liz Doren and Drue Assiter
www.emeraldkingdom.org

The Harvey Milk Foundation
www.milkfoundation.org

Q Center
Portland's LGBTQ Community Center
pdxqcenter.org

Wiki Queer
Web-based, not for profit, free-content
encyclopedia and resource hub project based
on an openly editable model, specifically for
and by the LGBTQ and ally communities
www.wikiqueer.org

Special Thanks

Andy Lorenz, Greg Kerr - Portland insights
Barbara "Babs" Finerman Bale Williams - Momma Bear
Becky Adams
Bella da Ball
Bill Sanderson - Foreword and BMB
Bill Stewart - Atlanta insights
Brad Roberts and Charger Stone - Washington DC insights
Brent Cage - London and international travel insights
Charles and Ray Eames
Cougar Garcia - Barcelona insights
Dave Gonzalez - TV Guide Channel
Dave Hernandez - Leather wardrobe
Dean Stevens
Dick and Irene Hacker
Doug Bale
Dwayne Bisbee - Dallas insights
Emily Abraham
Freezietooth - Marly and Rosie
Gavin Derek - Seattle insights
Harvey Milk
Jack Bale and Stephanie Wilson
Jay and Steve Crandall - West Hollywood insights
Jean Krikorian - Bear and Wolf room and board
Jennifer Tough Hemsley - Pixelita Press
Jon Stoa - San Francisco insights
Julie Hill - DC insights
Just for Men - Mustache and Beard dye
Karelle Levy - Miami insights
Kathy Griffin
Kristine Kunego - hostess w/ the mostess and pop-up shop girl Friday
Larry Smith
Linda Hesh - DC insights
Mark Rawley - London insights and Provincetown support
Marty Sarussi - Chicago insights
Matthew Reader - G.A.Y. Insights
Michael Wiener, Mark Bracero, Ken Glass and Pamela Barsky - NYC insights
Neely O'Hara
Patrick & Tom Boyd-Lloyd - Dallas insights
Pat Weikle - Atlanta insights
Paul Grossman and Randall McCormack - Philadelphia insights
Paul Highfield - Chicago insights
Peter Jirak - Design Wolf's intro inspiration
Randall Robinson - Ft. Lauderdale insights
Redmond: Her Majesty, the Princess Ladybeagle
Rich Lopez - Dallas Voice
Schmidget - mascot extraordinaire
Scott McGillivray - Ad Design
Simone Campbell - Host of "Urban Fringe" on FCC Free Radio
Steve Critcher - Leather wardrobe
Steve and Jerry Stevens
Stuart Comer - London insights
Will O'Bryan - Metro Weekly
Wil & Molly - Wolfly fashions
and... The Hollywood Foreign Press

GUIDE FOR THE

MODERN
BEAR

A FIELD STUDY of BEARS in the WILD
By Travis Smith and Chris Bale

Find ModernBear on

Valley of the
Bears

modern design+bears+retro+beefcake=

MODERN
BEAR
www.ModernBear.net

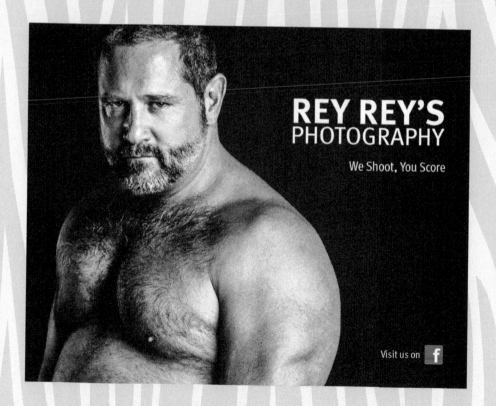

Leland Gebhardt
P H O T O G R A P H Y

lelandphotos.com

just modern
New Century Modern

901 N. Palm Canyon Dr., #105   Palm Springs, CA 92262
(760) 322-5600

justmoderndecor.com

THE BIGGEST HAIRIEST BEEFIEST BURLIEST CRAZIEST LAZIEST WEEKEND OF FUNDRAISING ON THE PLANET.

WWW.LAZYBEARWEEKEND.COM

JASON HILL DESIGN

Art / Design / Illustration

www.JasonHillDesign.com

Book design and illustration by Jason Hill
Photography by Leland Gebhardt
Hipstamatic photos by Chris Bale
Edited by Michelina Matarrese

Created by Modern Bear Media
Palm Springs, California, USA

www.facebook.com/modernbear
www.modernbear.net

CPSIA information can be obtained at www.ICGtesting.com
Printed in the USA
BVOW11s0424030714

358083BV00005B/18/P